Great Singers on the Art of Singing

HARRIETTE BROWER
AND
JAMES FRANCIS COOKE

DOVER PUBLICATIONS, INC.
Mineola, New York

Copyright

Published in Canada by General Publishing Company, Ltd., 30 Lesmill Road, Don Mills, Toronto, Ontario.

Published in the United Kingdom by Constable and Company, Ltd., 3 The Lanchesters, 162–164 Fulham Palace Road, London W6 9ER.

Bibliographical Note

This Dover edition, first published in 1996, is a new compilation of unabridged, slightly corrected chapters selected from two books: *Vocal Mastery: Talks with Master Singers and Teachers / Comprising Interviews with Caruso, Farrar, Maurel, Lehmann, and Others / by Harriette Brower*, originally published by Frederick A. Stokes Company Publishers, New York, 1920; and *Great Singers on the Art of Singing: Educational Conferences with Foremost Artists / by James Francis Cooke / A Series of Personal Study Talks with the Most Renowned Opera, Concert and Oratorio Singers of the Time / Especially Planned for Voice Students*, originally published by Theo. Presser Co., Philadelphia, Pa., 1921.

The Dover edition adds a list of contents, new chapter headings and a few footnotes to help clarify names and terms in the original texts. With two exceptions, singers' photographs, now grouped on pp. 149–154, prefaced each chapter in the original publications. The photographs of Lilli Lehmann and Herbert Witherspoon appeared in *The Great Opera Stars in Historic Photographs: 343 Portraits from the 1850's to the 1940's*, edited by James Camner, originally published by Dover Publications, Inc., 1978.

Library of Congress Cataloging-in-Publication Data

Great singers on the art of singing/Harriette Brower and James Francis Cooke.
     p.   cm.
    This ed. contains selected interviews from Brower's Vocal mastery and selected articles from Cooke's compilation Great singers on the art of singing.
    First work originally published: New York : Frederick A. Stokes Co., 1920; 2nd work originally published: Philadelphia : Theo. Presser Co., 1921.
    ISBN 0-486-29190-1 (pbk.)
    1. Singing. 2. Singers. I. Brower, Harriette, 1869–1928.
II. Cooke, James Francis, 1875–1960.
MT820.G8 1996
783—dc20
                                     96-25683
                                          CIP
                                         MN

Manufactured in the United States of America
Dover Publications, Inc., 31 East 2nd Street, Mineola, N.Y. 11501

Publisher's Note, 1996

This Dover edition consists of selected chapters from Harriette Brower's *Vocal Mastery* and James Francis Cooke's *Great Singers on the Art of Singing*. Selections from the Brower book take the form of interviews with singers and master teachers, and are so identified in those chapter headings. Selections from the Cooke volume consist of articles written by the artists themselves, each preceded by a biographical sketch by Cooke, set off typographically in square brackets.

Both Cooke's "Introduction," which opens the Dover edition and sets its overall tone, and Brower's "The Coda," which summarizes major lesson points, contain a few references to people included in the authors' original publications but omitted here. Those omissions reflect either unwanted duplication of lesson materials and commentary among the contributors or articles considered by the publisher to be less significant or less interesting to the reader.

Contents

Introduction

by

JAMES FRANCIS COOKE

VOCAL GOLD MINES AND HOW THEY ARE DEVELOPED

Plutarch tells how a Laconian youth picked all the feathers from the scrawny body of a nightingale and when he saw what a tiny thing was left exclaimed,

> *"Surely thou art all voice*
> *and nothing else!"*

Among the tens of thousands of young men and women who, having heard a few famous singers, suddenly determine to follow the trail of the footlights, there must be a very great number who think that the success of the singer is "voice and nothing else." If this collection of conferences serves to indicate how much more goes into the development of the modern singer than mere voice, the effort will be fruitful.

Nothing is more fascinating in human relations than the medium of communication we call speech. When this is combined with beautiful music in song, its charm is supreme. The conferences collected in this book were secured during a period of from ten to fifteen years; and in every case the notes have been carefully, often microscopically, reviewed and approved by the artist. They are the record of actual accomplishment and not mere metempirical opinions. The general design was directed by the hundreds of questions that had been presented to the writer in his own experience in teaching the art of singing. Only the practical teacher of singing has the opportunity to discover the real needs of the student; and only the artist of wide experience can answer many of the serious questions asked.

The writer's first interest in the subject of voice commenced with the recollection of the wonderfully human and fascinating vocal organ of Henry Ward Beecher, whom he had the joy to know in his early boyhood. The memory of such a voice as that of Beecher is ineradicable. Once, at the same age, he was taken to hear Beecher's rival pulpit orator, the Rev. T. de Witt Talmadge, in the Brooklyn Tabernacle. The harsh, raucous, nasal, penetrating, rasping, irritating voice of that clergyman only served to emphasize the delight in listening to Beecher. Then he heard the wonderful orotund organ of Col. Robert J. Ingersoll and the sonorous, mellow voice of Edwin Booth.

Shortly he found himself enlisted as a soprano in the boy choir of a large Episcopal church. While there he became the soloist, singing many of the leading arias from famous oratorios before he was able to identify the musical importance of such works. Then came a long training in piano and in organ playing, followed by public appearances as a pianist and engagements as an organist and choirmaster in different churches. This, coupled with song composition, musical criticism and editing, experience in conducting, managing concerts, accompanying noted singers and, later, in teaching voice for many years, formed a background that is recounted here only to let the reader know that the conferences were not put down by one unacquainted with the actual daily needs of the student, from his earliest efforts to his platform triumphs.

What Must the Singer Have?

What must the singer have? A voice? Of course. But how good must that voice be? "Ah, there's the rub!" It is this very point which adds so much fascination to the chances of becoming a great singer; and it is this very point upon which so many, many careers have been wrecked. The young singer learns that Jenny Lind was first refused by Garcia because he considered her case hopeless; he learns that Sir George Henschel told Bispham that he had insufficient voice to encourage him to take up the career of the singer; he learns dozens of similar instances; and then he goes to hear some famous singer with slender vocal gifts who, by force of tremendous dramatic power, eclipses dozens with finer voices. He thereupon resolves that "voice" must be a secondary matter in the singer's success.

There could not be a greater mistake. There must be a good vocal basis. There must be a voice capable of development through a sufficient gamut to encompass the great works written for such a voice. It must be capable of development into sufficient "size" and power that it may fill large auditoriums. It must be sweet, true to pitch, clear; and, above all, it must have that kind of an individual quality which seems to draw the musical interest of the average person to it.

The Perfect Voice

Paradoxically enough, the public does not seem to want the "perfect" voice, but rather, the "human" voice. A noted expert, who for many years directed the recording laboratories of a famous sound reproducing machine company, a man whose acquaintance with great singers of the time is very wide, once told the writer of a singer who made records so perfect from the standpoint of tone that no musical critic could possibly find fault with them. Yet these records did not meet with a market from the general public. The reason is that the public demands something far more than a flawless voice and technically correct singing. It demands the human quality, that wonderful something that shines through the voice of every normal, living being as the soul shines through the eyes. It is this thing which gives individuality and identity to the voice and makes the widest appeal to the greatest number of people.

Patti was not great because her dulcet tones were like honey to the ear. Mere sweetness does not attract vast audiences time and again. Once, in a mediæval German city, the writer was informed that a nightingale had been heard in the *glacis* on the previous night. The following evening a party of friends was formed and wandered through the park whispering with delight at every outburst from the silver throat. Never had bird music been so beautiful. The next night someone suggested that we go again; but no one could be found who was enthusiastic enough to repeat the experience. The very perfection of the nightingale's song, once heard, had been sufficient.

THE LURE OF INDIVIDUALITY

Certain performers in vaudeville owe their continued popularity to the fascinating individuality of their voices. Albert Chevalier, once heard, could never be forgotten. His pathetic lilt to "My old Dutch" has made thousands weep. When he sings such a number he has a far higher artistic control over his audience than many an elaborately trained singer trilling away at some very complicated aria.

A second-rate opera singer once bemoaned his fate to the writer. He complained that he was obliged to sing for $100.00 a week, notwithstanding his years of study and preparation, while Harry Lauder, the Scotch comedian, could get $1000 a night on his tours. As a matter of fact Mr. Lauder, entirely apart from his ability as an actor, had a far better voice and had that appealing quality that simply commandeers his auditors the moment he opens his mouth.

Any method or scheme of teaching the art of singing that does not seek to develop the inherent intellectual and emotional vocal complexion of the singer can never approach a good method. Vocal perfection that does not admit of the manifestation of the real individual has been the death knell of many an aspiring student. Nordica, Jean de Reszke, Victor Maurel, Plançon, Sims Reeves, Schumann-Heink, Garden, Dr. Wüllner, Evan Williams, Galli-Curci, and especially our greatest of American singers, David Bispham, all have manifested a vocal individuality as unforgetable to the ear as their countenances are to the eye.

If the reader happens to be a young singer and can grasp the significance of the previous paragraph, he may have something more valuable to him than many lessons. The world is not seeking merely the perfect voice but a great musical individuality manifested through a voice developed to express that individuality in the most natural and at the same time the most comprehensive manner possible. Therefore, young man and young woman, does it not seem of the greatest importance to you to develop, first of all, the *mind and the soul,* so that when the great hour comes, your audience will hear through the notes that pour from your throat something of your intellectual and emotional character? They will not know how, nor will they ask why they hear it—but its manifestation will either be there or it will not be there. Upon this will depend much of your future success. It can not be concealed from the discerning critics in whose hands your progress rests. The high intellectual training received in college by Ffrangçon Davies, David Bispham, Plunkett Greene, Herbert Witherspoon, Reinald Werrenrath and others, is just as apparent to the intelligent listener, in their singing at recitals, as it would be in their conversation. Others have received an equivalent intellectual training in other ways. The young singer, who thinks that in the future he can "get by" without such a training, is booked for disappointment. Get a college education if you can; and, if you can not, fight to get its equivalent. No useful experience in the singer's career is a wasted one. The early instrumental training of Melba, Sembrich, Campanari, Hempel, Dalmores, Garden, and Galli-Curci, shows out in their finished singing, in wonderful manner. Every singer should be able to play the piano well. It has a splendid effect in the musical discipline of the mind. In European conservatories, in many instances, the study of the piano is compulsory.

YOUR PHILOSOPHY OF SINGING

The student of singing should be an inveterate reader of "worthwhile" comments upon his art. In this way, if he has a discriminating mind, he will be able to form a "philosophy of singing" of his own. Richard Wagner prefaced his music dramas with lengthy essays giving his reasons for pursuing a certain course. Whatever their value may be to the musical public at this time, it could not have been less than that to the great master when he was fighting to straighten out for his own satisfaction in his own mind just what he should do and how he should do it. Therefore, read interminably; but believe nothing that you read until you have weighed it carefully in your own mind and determined its usefulness in its application to your own particular case.

The student will find the following books of real value in his quest for vocal truth: *The Philosophy of Singing,* Clara Kathleen Rogers; *The Vocal Instructor,* E. J. Myer; *The Psychology of Singing,* David C. Taylor; *How to*

Sing, Lilli Lehmann; *Reminiscences of a Quaker Singer*, David Bispham; *The Art of the Singer*, W. J. Henderson.

The student should also read the biographies of famous singers and keep in touch with the progress of the art, through reading the best magazines.

THE HISTORY OF SINGING

The history of singing parallels the history of civilization. Egypt, Israel, Greece and Rome made their contributions; but how they sang and what they sang we can not definitely know because of the destruction of the bridge between ancient and modern notation, and because not until Thomas Edison invented the phonograph in 1877 was there any tangible means of recording the voices of the singers. The wisdom of Socrates, Plato and Caesar is therefore of trifling significance in helping us to find out more than how highly the art was regarded. The absurd antics of Nero, in his ambition to distinguish himself as a singer, indicated in some more or less indefinite way the importance given to singing in the heyday of Rome. The incessant references to singing, in Greek literature, tell us that singing was looked upon not merely as an accomplishment but as one of the necessary arts.

Coincident with the coming of Italian opera, about 1600, we find a great revival of the art of singing; and many of the old Italian masters have bequeathed us some fairly instructive comments upon the art of *bel canto*. That these old Italian teachers were largely individualists and taught empirically, with no set methods other than that which their own ears determined, seems to be accepted quite generally by investigators at this date. The *Osservazione sopra il Canto figurato* of Pietro Francesco Tosi (procurable in English), published in 1723, and the *Reflessioni pratiche sul Canto figurato*, published in 1776, are valuable documents for the serious student, particularly because these men seemed to recognize that the so-called registers should be equalized. With them developed an ever-expanding jargon of voice directions which persist to this day among vocal teachers. Such directions as "sing through the mask" (meaning the face); "sing with the throat open"; "sing as though you were just about to smile"; "sing as though you were just about to experience the sensation of swallowing" (*come bere*); "support the tone"; etc., etc., are often more confusing than helpful. Manual García (1805–1906), who invented the laryngoscope in 1855, made an earnest effort to bring scientific observation to the aid of the vocal teacher, by providing a tiny mirror on the end of a rod, enabling the teacher to see the vocal cords during the process of phonation. How much this actually helped the singing teacher is still a moot point; but it must be remembered that García had many extremely successful pupils, including the immortal Jenny Lind.

The writer again advises the serious student of singing to spend a great deal of time in forming his own conception of the principles by which he can get the most from his voice. Any progressive artist teacher will encourage him in this course. In other words, it is not enough in these days that he shall sing; but he must know how he produces his results and be able to produce them time and time again with constantly increasing success. Note in the succeeding conferences how many of the great singers have given very careful and minute consideration to this. The late Evan Williams spent years of thought and study upon it; and the writer considers that his observations in this volume are among the most important contributions to the literature of voice teaching. This was the only form in which they appeared in print. Only one student in a hundred thousand can dispense with a good vocal teacher, as did the brilliant Galli-Curci or the unforgetable Campanari. A really fine teacher of voice is practically indispensable to most students. This does not mean that the best teacher is the one with the greatest reputation. The reputation of a teacher only too often has depended upon his good fortune early in life in securing pupils who have made spectacular successes in a short time. There are hundreds of splendid vocal teachers in America now, and it is very gratifying to see many of their pupils make great successes in Europe without any previous instruction "on the other side."

Surely nothing can be more helpful to the ambitious vocal student than the direct advice, personal suggestions and hints of the greatest singers of the time. It is with this thought that the writer takes especial pride in being the medium of the presentation of the following conferences. It is suggested that a careful study of the best sound-reproducing-machine records of the great singers included will add much to the interest of the study of this work.

The enormous incomes received from some vocal gold mines, such as Caruso, John McCormack, Patti, Galli-Curci, and others, have made the lure of the singer's career so great that many young vocalists are inclined to forget that all of the great singers of the day have attained their triumphs only after years of hard work. Galli-Curci's overwhelmingly successful American debut followed years of real labor, when she was glad to accept small engagements in order to advance in her art. John McCormack's first American appearances were at a side show at the St. Louis World's Fair. Sacrifice is often the seed kernel of large success. Too few young singers are willing to plant that kernel. They expect success to come at the end of a few courses of study and a few hundred dollars spent in advertising. The public, particularly the American public, is a wary one. It may be possible to advertise worthless gold mining stock in such a way that thousands may be swindled before the crook behind the scheme is jailed. But it is impossible to sell our public a so-called golden-voiced singer whose voice is really nothing more than tin-foil and very thin tin-foil at that.

Every year certain kinds of slippery managers accept huge fees from would-be singers, which are supposed to be invested in a mysterious formula which, like the philosopher's stone, will turn a baser metal into pure gold. No campaign of advertising spent upon a mediocrity or an inadequately prepared artist can ever result in anything but a disastrous waste. Don't spend a penny in advertising until you have really something to sell which the public will want. It takes years to make a fine singer known; but it takes only one concert to expose an inadequate singer. Every one of the artists represented in this book has been "through the mill" and every one has triumphed gloriously in the end. There is one road. They have defined it in remarkable fashion in these conferences. The sign-posts read, "Work, Sacrifice, Joy, Triumph."

With the multiplicity of methods and schemes for practice it is not surprising that the main essentials of the subject are sometimes obscured. That such discussions as those included in this book will enable the thinking student to crystallize in his own mind something which to him will become a method long after he has left his student days, can not be questioned. One of the significant things which he will have to learn is perfect intonation, keeping on the right pitch all the time; and another thing is freedom from restriction, best expressed by the word poise. William Shakespeare, greatest of English singing teachers of his day, once expressed these important points in the following words:

"The Foundations of the Art of Singing are two in number:

"First: (A) How to take breath and (B) how to press it out slowly. (The act of slow exhalation is seen in our endeavor to warm some object with the breath.)

"Second: How to sing to this controlled breath pressure.

"It may be interesting at this point to observe how the old singers practiced when seeking a full tone while using little breath. They watched the effect of their breath by singing against a mirror or against the flame of a taper. If a note required too much pressure the command over the breath was lost—the mirror was unduly tarnished or the flame unduly puffed. 'Ah' was their pattern vowel, being the most difficult on account of the openness of the throat—the vowel which, by letting more breath out, demanded the greatest control. The perfect poise of the instrument on the controlled breath was found to bring about *three* important results to the singer:

"*First result*—Unerring tuning. As we do not experience any sensation of consciously using the muscles in the throat, we can only judge of the result by listening. When the note sounds to the right breath control it springs unconsciously and instantaneously to the tune we intended. The freedom of the instrument not being interfered with, it follows through our wishing it—like any other act naturally performed. This unerring tuning is the first result of a right foundation.

"*Second result*—The throat spaces are felt to be unconscious and arrange themselves independently in the different positions prompted by the will and necessary to pronounciation, the factors being freedom of tongue and soft palate, and freedom of lips.

"*Third result*—The complete freedom of the face and eyes which adapt themselves to those changes necessary to the expression of the emotions.

"The artist can increase the intensity of his tone without necessarily increasing its volume, and can thus produce the softest effect. By his skill he can emit the soft note and cause it to travel as far as a loud note, thus arousing emotions as of distance, as of memories of the past. He produces equally well the more powerful gradations without overstepping the boundary of noble and expressive singing. On the other hand, an indifferent performer would scarcely venture on a soft effect, the absence of breath support would cause him to become inaudible and should he attempt to crescendo such a note the result would be throaty and unsatisfactory."

Another most important subject is diction, and the writer can think of nothing better than to quote from Mme. Lilli Lehmann, the greatest Wagnerian soprano of the last century:

"Let us now consider some of the reasons why some American singers have failed to succeed. How do American women begin their studies? Many commence their lessons in December or January. They take two or three half-hour lessons a week, even attending these irregularly, and ending their year's instruction in March or, at the latest, in April. Surely music study under such circumstances is little less than farcical. The voice, above all things, needs careful and constant attention. Moreover, many are lacking lamentably in the right preparations. Some are evidently so benighted as to believe that preparation is unnecessary. Or do they believe that the singing teacher must also provide a musical and general education?

"Is there one among them, for instance, who can enunciate her own language faultlessly; that is, as the stage demands? Many fail to realize that they should, first of all, be taught elocution (diction) by teachers who can show them how to pronounce vowels purely and beautifully, and consonants correctly and distinctly, so as to give words their proper sounds. How can anyone expect to sing in a foreign language when he has no idea of his own language—no idea how this wonderful member, the tongue, should be used—to say nothing of the terrible faults in speaking? I endorse the study of elocution as a preparatory study for all singing. No one can realize how much simpler and how much more efficient it would make the work of the singing teacher."

Finally, the writer feels that there is much to be inferred from the popular criticism of the man in the street—"There is no music in that voice." Mr. Hoi-polloi knows just what he means when he says that. As a matter of fact, the average voice has very little music in it. By music the man means that the pitch of the tones that he hears shall be so unmistakable and so accurate, that the quality shall be so pure and the thought of the singer so sincere and so worth-while, that the auditor feels the wonderful human emotion that comes only from listening to a beautiful human voice. Put real music in every tone and your success will not be far distant.

What the American Girl Should Know About an Operatic Career

by

FRANCES ALDA

[Biographical sketch by James Francis Cooke]

[Mme. Frances Alda was born at Christ Church, New Zealand, May 31st, 1883. She was educated at Melbourne and studied singing with Mathilde Marchesi in Paris. Her debut was made in Massenet's *Manon,* at the Opéra Comique in Paris in 1904. After highly successful engagements in Paris, Brussels, Parma and Milan (where she created the title role in the Italian version of *Louise*), she made her American debut at the Metropolitan Opera House in New York as Gilda in Verdi's *Rigoletto.* Since her initial success in New York she has been connected with the Metropolitan stage every season. In 1910 she married Giulio Gatti-Casazza, manager of the Metropolitan Opera House, and is probably better able to speak upon the subject herewith discussed than any one in America. She has also appeared with great success in London, Warsaw, Buenos Aires and other cities, in opera and in concert. Many of the most important leading roles in modern opera have been created by her in America.]

REGULARITY AND SUCCESS

To the girl who aspires to have an operatic career, who has the requisite vocal gifts, physical health, stage presence and—most important of all—a high degree of intelligence, the great essential is regular daily work. This implies regular lessons, regular practice, regular exercise, regular sleep, regular meals— in fact, a life of regularity. The daily lesson in most cases seems an imperative necessity. Lessons strung over a series of years merely because it seems more economical to take one lesson a week instead of seven rarely produce the expected results. Marchesi, with her famous wisdom on vocal matters, advised twenty minutes a day and then not more than ten minutes at a time.

For nine months I studied with the great Parisian maestra and in my tenth month I made my debut. Of course, I had sung a great deal before that time and also could play both the piano and the violin. A thorough musical knowledge is always valuable. The early years of the girl who is destined for an operatic career may be much more safely spent with Czerny exercises for the piano or Kreutzer studies for the violin than with Concone solfeggios for the voice. Most girls over-exercise their voices during the years when they are too delicate. It always pays to wait and spend the time in developing the purely musical side of study.

MODERATION AND GOOD SENSE

More voices collapse from over-practice and more careers collapse from under-work than from anything else. The girl who hopes to become a prima donna will dream of her work morning, noon and night. Nothing can take it out of her mind. She will seek to study every imaginable thing that could in any way contribute to her equipment. There is so much to learn that she must work hard to learn all. Even now I study pretty regularly two hours a day, but I rarely sing more than a few minutes. I hum over my new roles with my accompanist, Frank La Forge, and study them in that way. It was to such methods as this that Marchesi attributed the wonderful longevity of the voices of her best-known pupils. When they followed the advice of the dear old maestra their voices lasted a long, long time. Her vocal exercises were little more than scales sung very slowly, single, sustained tones repeated time and again until her critical ear was entirely satisfied, and then arpeggios. After that came more complicated technical drills to prepare the pupil for the fioriture work demanded in the more florid operas. At the base of all, however, were the simplest kind of exercises. Through her discriminating sense of tone quality, her great persistence and her boundless enthusiasm, she used these simple vocal materials with a wizardry that produced great *prime donne*.

THE PRECIOUS HEAD VOICE

Marchesi laid great stress upon the use of the head voice. This she illustrated to all her pupils herself, at the same time not hesitating to insist that it was impossible for a male teacher to teach the head voice properly. (Marchesi herself carried out her theories by refusing to teach any male applicants.) She never let any pupil sing above F on the top line of the treble staff in anything but the head voice. They rarely ever touched their highest notes with full voice. The upper part of the voice was conserved with infinite care to avoid early breakdowns. Even when the pupils sang the top notes they did it with the feeling that there was still something in reserve. In my operatic work at present I feel this to be of greatest importance. The singer who exhausts herself upon the top notes is neither artistic nor effective.

THE AMERICAN GIRL'S CHANCES IN OPERA

The American girl who fancies that she has less chances in opera than her sisters of the European countries is silly. Look at the lists of artists at the Metropolitan, for instance. The list includes twice as many artists of American nationality as of any other nation. This is in no sense the result of pandering to the patriotism of the American public. It is simply a matter of supply and demand. New Yorkers demand the best opera in the world and expect the best voices in the world. The management would accept fine artists with fine voices from China or Africa or the North Pole if they were forthcoming. A diamond is a diamond no matter where it comes from. The management virtually ransacks the musical marts of Europe every year for fine voices. Inevitably the list of American artists remains higher. On the whole, the American girls have better natural voices, more ambition and are willing to study seriously, patiently and energetically. This is due in a measure to better physical conditions in America and in Australia, another free country that has produced unusual singers. What is the result? America is now producing the best and enjoying the best. There is more fine music of all kinds now in New York during one week than one can get in Paris in a month and more than one can get in Milan in six months. This has made New York a great operatic and musical center. It is a wonderful opportunity for Americans who desire to enter opera.

THE NEED FOR SUPERIOR INTELLIGENCE

There was a time in the halcyon days of the old coloratura singers when the opera singer was not expected to have very much more intelligence than a parrot. Any singer who could warble away at runs and trills was a great artist. The situation has changed entirely today. The modern operagoer demands great acting as well as great singing. The opera house calls for brains as well as voices. There should properly be great and sincere rivalry among fine singers. The singer must listen to other singers with minute care and patience, and then try to learn how to improve herself by self-study and intelligent comparison. Just as the great actor studies everything that pertains to his role, so the great singer knows the history of the epoch of the opera in which he is to appear, he knows the customs, he may know something of the literature of the time. In other words, he must live and think in another atmosphere before he can walk upon the stage and make the audience feel that he is really a part of the picture. Sir Herbert Beerbohm Tree gave a presentation that was convincing and beautiful, while the mediocre actor, not willing to give as much brain work to his performance, falls far short of an artistic performance.

A modern performance of any of the great works as they are presented at the Metropolitan is rehearsed with great care and attention to historical detail. Instances of this are the performances of *L'Amore dei Tre Re, Carmen, Bohême,* and *Lohengrin,* as well as such great works as *Die Meistersinger* and *Tristan und Isolde.*

PHYSICAL STRENGTH AND SINGING

Few singers seem to realize that an operatic career will be determined in its success very largely through physical strength, all other factors being present in the desired degree. That is, the singer must be strong physically in order to succeed in opera. This applies to women as well as to men. No one knows what the physical strain is, how hard the work and study are. In front of you is a sea of highly intelligent, cultured people, who for years have been trained in the best traditions of the opera. They pay the highest prices paid anywhere for entertainment. They are entitled to the best. To face such an audience and maintain the high traditions of the house through three hours of a complicated modern score is a musical, dramatic and in-tellectual feat that demands, first of all, a superb physical condition. Every day of my life in New York I go for a walk, mostly around the reservoir in Central Park, because it is high and the air is pure and free. As a result I seldom have a cold, even in midwinter. I have not missed a performance in eight years, and this, of course, is due to the fact that my health is my first daily consideration.

The Message of the Singer

An interview with

MARGUERITE D'ALVAREZ

by Harriette Brower

A great podium backed with green, reminding one of a forest of palms; dim lights through the vast auditorium; a majestic, black-robed figure standing alone among the palms, pouring out her voice in song; a voice at once vibrant, appealing, powerful, filled now with sweeping passion, again with melting tenderness; such was the stage setting for my first impression of Mme. Marguerite d'Alvarez, and such were some of the emotions she conveyed.

Soon after this experience, I asked if I might have a personal talk with the artist whose singing had made such a deep impression upon me. It was most graciously granted, and at the appointed hour I found myself in a charmingly appointed yet very homelike salon, chatting with this Spanish lady from Peru, who speaks such beautiful English and is courtesy itself.

This time it was not a somber, black-robed figure who came forward so graciously to greet me, for above a black satin walking skirt, Madame had added a blouse of soft creamy lace, which revealed the rounded curves of neck and arms; the only ornament being a string of pearls about the full throat. Later in our talk I ventured to express my preference for creamy draperies instead of black, for the concert room; but the singer thought otherwise. "No," she said; "my gown must be absolutely unobtrusive—negative. I must not use it to heighten effect, or to attract the audience to me personally. People must be drawn to me by what I express, by my art, by what I have to give them."

But to begin at the beginning. In answer to my first question, "What must one do to become a singer?" Madame said:

"To become a singer, one must have a voice; that is of the first importance. In handling and training that voice, breathing is perhaps the most vital thing to be considered. To some breath control seems to be second nature; others must toil for it. With me it is intuition; it has always been natural. Breathing is such an individual thing. With each person it is different, for no two people breathe in just the same way, whether natural or acquired. Just as one pianist touches the keys of the instrument in his own peculiar way, unlike the ways of all other pianists. For instance, no two singers will deliver the opening phrase of 'My heart at thy sweet voice,' from *Samson,* in exactly the same way. One will expend a little more breath on some tones than on others; one may sing it softer, another louder. Indeed how can two people ever give out a phrase in the same way, when they each feel it differently? The great thing is to control the management of the breath through intelligent study. But alas,"—with a pretty little deprecating gesture—"many singers do not seem to use their intelligence in the right way. They need to study so many things besides vocalises and a few songs. They ought to broaden themselves in every way. They should know books, pictures, sculpture, acting, architecture—in short everything possible in the line of art, and of life. For all these things will help them to sing more intelligently. They should cultivate all these means of self-expression. For myself, I have had a liberal education in music—piano, harmony, theory, composition and kindred subjects. And then I love and study art in all its forms and manifestations."

"Your first recital in New York was a rich and varied feast," I remarked.

"Indeed I feel I gave the audience too much; there was such a weight of meaning to each song, and so many! I cannot sing indifferent or superficial songs. I must sing those which mean much, either of sadness or mirth, passion or exaltation. No one knows (who has not been through it) what it means to face a great audience of strangers, knowing that something in you must awake those people and draw them toward you: you must bare your very soul to them and bring theirs to you, in answering response, just by your voice. It is a wonderful thing, to bring to masses of people a message in this way. I feel this strongly, whenever I stand before a large audience, that with every note I sing I am delivering something of the God-given gift which has been granted to me—that I can do some good to each one who hears. If they do not care for me, or if they misunderstand my message, they may hate me—at first. When they do understand, then they adore me.

SENTIMENT VERSUS TEMPERAMENT

"You can well believe it is far more difficult to sing a recital program than to do an operatic role. In the recital you are absolutely alone, and entirely responsible for your effect on the audience. You must be able to express every variety of emotion and feeling, must make them realize the difference between sorrow and happiness, revenge or disdain; in short, make them, for the moment, experience these things. The artist who can best vivify these varying emotions must have temperament. On the piano, you may hear players who express sentiment, feeling, fine discrimination in tone color and shading; but comparatively few possess real temperament. There is a great difference between that quality and sentiment. The one can be learned, to a certain extent; but temperament is one's very life and soul, and is bound to sweep everything before it. Of this one thing I am very sure; the singer cannot express all these emotions without feeling them to the full during performance. I always feel every phrase I sing—I live it. That is why, after a long and exhausting program, I am perfectly limp and spent. For I have given all that was in me. Friends of Sarah Bernhardt say that after a performance, they would find her stretched prone on a couch in her dressing room, scarcely able to move or speak. The strain of a public appearance, when one gives one's heart's blood, is beyond words"; and Madame's upturned face and expressive gesture denoted how keenly alive she was to this experience.

After a little pause, I said: "Let us come down to earth, while you tell me just how you study. No doubt you do some daily technical practice."

MASSAGE THE VOICE

"Oh, yes, technic is most important; one can do nothing without it. When I begin to study in the morning, I give the voice what I call a massage. One's voice cannot be driven, it must be coaxed, enticed. This massage consists of humming exercises, with closed lips. Humming is the sunshine of the voice." The singer illustrated the idea with a short musical figure, consisting of three consecutive tones of the diatonic scale, ascending and descending several times; on each repetition the phrase began on the next higher note of the scale. "You see," she continued, "this little exercise brings the tone fully forward. As you feel the vibration, it should be directly between the eyes.

"Now, after you have coaxed the voice forward in this way, and then opened your lips to sing a full tone, this tone should, indeed must, be right in the same place where the humming tones were—it cannot be anywhere else." Madame illustrated again, first humming on one tone, then letting it out with full resonance, using the vowel "ah," which melted into "o," and later changed into "u," as the tone died away. "This vibration in the voice should not be confounded with a tremolo, which is, of course, very undesirable. A voice without vibrato would be cold and dead, expressionless. There must be this pulsing quality in the tone, which carries waves of feeling on it.

"Thus the singer entices the voice to come forward and out, never treating it roughly or harshly, never forcing or straining it. Take pleasure in every tone you make; with patience and pleasure much is accomplished. I could not give you a more useful tip than this."

"Will you tell me how you learn a song?" she was asked.

"I first read over the text and get a good idea of its meaning. When I begin to study the song, I never separate the music from the words, but learn both together. I play the piano of course, and thus can get a good idea of the accompaniment, and of the whole *ensemble.*

"I feel so strongly that real art, the highest art, is for those who truly understand it and its mission. A dream of mine is one day to found a school of true art. Everything in this school shall be on a high plane of thought. The instructors shall be gifted themselves and have only lofty ideals. And it will be such a happiness to watch the development of talent which may blossom into genius through having the right nurture. I shall watch this work from a distance, for I might be too anxious if I allowed myself to be in the midst of the work. But this is my dream, and I hope it will one day come true."

Modern Vocal Methods in Italy

by

PASQUALE AMATO

[Biographical sketch by James Francis Cooke]

[Pasquale Amato, for so many years the leading baritone at the Metropolitan Opera House in New York, was born at Naples March 21st, 1878. He was intended for the career of an engineer and was educated at the Instituto Tecnico Domenico. He then studied at the Conservatory of Naples from 1896 to 1899. His teachers there were Cucialla and Carelli. He made his debut as Germont in *La Traviata* in the Teatro Bellini at Naples in 1900. Thereafter his successes have been exceptionally great in the music centers of South America, Italy, Russia, England, Egypt, and Germany. He has created numerous roles at the Metropolitan Opera House, among them Jack Rance in *The Girl of the Golden West;* Golaud in *Pelleas and Melisande* (Milan); *L'Amore dei Tre Re; Cyrano* (Damrosch); *Lodoletta* (Mascagni); *Madame Sans Gêne*. He has visited South America as an artist no less than ten times. His voice is susceptible of fine dramatic feeling.]

When I was about sixteen years of age my voice was sufficiently settled to encourage my friends and family to believe that I might become a singer. This is a proud discovery for an Italian boy, as singing—especially operatic singing—is held in such high regard in Italy that one naturally looks forward with joy to a career in the great opera houses of one's native country and possibly to those over the sea. At eighteen I was accordingly entered in the conservatory, but not without many conditions, which should be of especial interest to young American vocal students. The teachers did not immediately accept me as good vocal material. I was recognized to have musical inclinations and musical gifts and I was placed under observation so that it might be determined whether the state-supported conservatory should direct my musical education along vocal lines or along other lines.

This is one of the cardinal differences between musical education in America and musical education in Italy. In America a pupil suddenly determines that he is destined to become a great opera singer and forthwith he hires a teacher to make him one. He might have been destined to become a plumber, or a lawyer, or a comedian, but that has little to do with the matter if he has money and can employ a teacher. In Italy such a direction of talents would be considered a waste to the individual and to the state. Of course the system has its very decided faults, for a corps of teachers with poor or biased judgment could do a great deal of damage by discouraging real talent, as was, indeed, the case with the great Verdi, who at the age of eighteen was refused admission to the Milan Conservatory by the director, Basili, on the score of lack of talent.

However, for the most part the judges are experienced and skilful men, and when a pupil has been under surveillance for some time the liability of an error in judgment is very slight. Accordingly, after I had spent some time in getting acquainted with music through the study of Notation, Sight-singing, Theory, Harmony, Piano, etc., I was informed at the end of two years that I had been selected for an operatic career. I can remember the time with great joy. It meant a new life to me, for I was certain that with the help of such conservative masters I should succeed.

On the whole, at this time, I consider the Italian system a very wise one for it does not fool away any time with incompetence. I have met so many young musicians who have shown indications of great study but who seem destitute of talent. It seems like coaxing insignificant shrubs to become great oak trees. No amount of coaxing or study will give them real talent if they do not have it, so why waste the money of the state and the money of the individual upon it. On the other hand, wherever in the world there is real talent, the state should provide money to develop it, just as it provides money to educate the young.

Italian Vocal Teaching

So much has been said about the Old Italian Vocal Method that the very name brings ridicule in some quarters. Nothing has been the subject for so much charlatanry. It is something that any teacher, good or bad, can claim in this country. Every Italian is of course very proud indeed of the wonderful vocal traditions of Italy, the centuries of idealism in search of better and better tone production. There are of course certain statements made by great voice teachers of other days that have been put down and may be read in almost any library in large American cities. But that these things make a vocal method that will suit all cases is too absurd to consider. The good sense of the old Italian Master would hold such a plan up to ridicule. Singing is first of all an art, and an art can not be circumscribed by any set of rules or principles.

The artist must, first of all, know a very great deal about all possible phases of the technic of his art and must then adjust himself to the particular problem before him. Therefore we might say that the Italian method was a method and then again that it was no method. As a matter of fact it is thousands of methods—one for each case or vocal problem. For instance, if I were to sing by the same means that Mr. Caruso employs it would not at all be the best thing for my voice, yet for Mr. Caruso it is without question the very best method, or his vocal quality would not be in such superb condition after constant years of use. He is the proof of his own method.

I should say that the Italian vocal teacher teaches, first of all, with his ears. He listens with the greatest possible intensity to every shade of tone-color until his ideal tone reveals itself. This often requires months and months of patience. The teacher must recognize the vocal deficiencies and work to correct them. For instance, I never had to work with my high tones. They are today produced in the same way in which I produced them when I was a boy. Fortunately I had teachers who recognized this and let it go at that.

Possibly the worst kind of a vocal teacher is the one who has some set plan or device or theory which must be followed "willy-nilly" in order that the teacher's theories may be vindicated. With such a teacher no voice is safe. The very best natural voices have to follow some patent plan just because the teacher has been taught in one way, is inexperienced, and has not good sense enough to let nature's perfect work alone. Both of my teachers knew that my high tones were all right and the practice was directed toward the lower tones. They worked me for over ten months on scales and sustained tones until the break that came at E flat above the bass clef was welded from the lower tones to the upper tones so that I could sing up or down with no ugly break audible.

I was drilled at first upon the vowel "ah." I hear American vocal authorities refer to "ah" as in *father*. That seems to me too flat a sound, one lacking in real resonance. The vowel used in my case in Italy and in hundreds of other cases I have noted is a slightly broader vowel, such as may be found half-way between the vowel "ah" as in *father,* and the "aw" as in *law.* It is not a dull sound, yet it is not the sound of "ah" in *father.* Perhaps the word "doff" or the first syllable of *Boston,* when properly pronounced, gives the right impression.

I do not know enough of American vocal training to give an intelligent criticism, but I wonder if American vocal teachers give as much attention to special parts of the training as teachers in Italy do. I hope they do, as I consider it very necessary. Consider the matter of staccato. A good vocal staccato is really a very difficult thing—difficult when it is right; that is, when on the pitch—every time, clear, distinct, and at the same time not hard and stiff. It took me weeks to acquire the right way of singing such a passage as *Un dì, quando le veneri,* from *Traviata,* but those were very profitable weeks—

Un dì, quan-do le   ve - ne-ri   il

tem-po a - vrà   fu - ga - te

Accurate attack in such a passage is by no means easy. Anyone can sing it—but *how it is sung* makes the real difference.

The public has very odd ideas about singing. For instance, it would be amazed to learn that *Trovatore* is a much more difficult role for me to sing and sing right than either *Parsifal* or *Pelleas and Melisande.* This largely because of the pure vocal demands and the flowing style. The Debussy opera, wonderful as it is, does not begin to make the vocal demands that such a work as *Trovatore* does.

When the singer once acquires proficiency, the acquisition of new roles comes very easy indeed. The main difficulty is the daily need for drilling the voice until it has the same quality every day. It can be done only by incessant attention. Here are some of the exercises I do every day with my accompanist:

First time forte, second time piano.

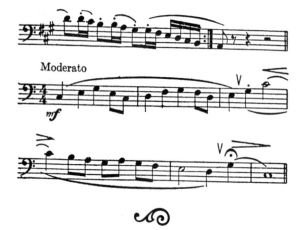

The Making of Artist Singers

An interview with

DAVID BISPHAM

by Harriette Brower

If we were asked to name one of the best known and best loved of American singers, the choice would surely fall on David Bispham. This artist, through his vocal, linguistic and histrionic gifts, his serious aims and high ideals, has endeared himself to musicians and music lovers alike. We are all proud of him as an American, and take a sort of personal pride in his achievements.

Mr. Bispham has been before the public as actor-singer for many years. There is no other artist in the English-speaking world who has had greater experience in all kinds of vocal work than this "Quaker Singer," as he calls himself, for he comes from Philadelphia, and is of old English, Quaker, Colonial stock. His professional debut was made in London, in 1891, with the Royal English Opera Company, as the Duc de Longueville in the beautiful opera comique, *The Basoche,* by Messager. The following year he appeared in Wagnerian music drama at the Royal Opera, Covent Garden, performing the part of Kurwenal, in *Tristan and Isolde,* without rehearsal. His adaptability to music in English, French, Italian and German caused him to be at once accepted as a member of that distinguished company.

In 1896, Mr. Bispham joined the forces of the Metropolitan Opera House, New York, and remained there for a number of years, singing each season alternately on both sides of the ocean. Of recent years he has devoted most of his time to concerts, though he is one of the founders and officers of the Society of American Singers, with which artistic body he frequently appears in the classic operas of Mozart, Pergolesi, Donizetti and others.

My first conference with Mr. Bispham was held in his New York studio. Here, in this artistic retreat where absolute quiet reigns, though located in the heart of the great city's busy life, the noted singer teaches and works out his programs and various characterizations.

THE PROBLEM OF BREATH CONTROL

"The singer should breathe as easily and naturally as animals and people do when they sleep," he began. "But we are awake when we sing; correct breath control, therefore, must be carefully studied, and is the result of understanding and experience. The best art conceals art. The aim is to produce tones with the utmost ease and naturalness, though these must be gained with patient toil. A child patting the keyboard with his tiny hands, is *unconsciously* natural and at ease, though he does not know what he is doing; the great pianist is *consciously* at ease because he understands principles of ease and relaxation, and has acquired the necessary control through years of training.

"The singer acquires management of the breath through correct position and action of his anatomy. The body is held erect, chest active; the network of abdominal muscles constantly gain strength as they learn to push, push, push the air up through the lungs to the windpipe, then through the mouth and nasal cavities." Mr. Bispham illustrated each point in his own person as he described it.

"When the manner of taking breath, and the way to develop the diaphragm and abdominal muscles, is understood, that is only a beginning. Management of the breath is an art in itself. The singer must know what to do with the breath once he has taken it in, or he may let it out in quarts the moment he opens his mouth. He has to learn how much he needs for each phrase. He learns how to conserve the breath; and while it is not desirable to hold one tone to attenuation, that the gallery may gasp with astonishment, as some singers do, yet it is well to learn to do all one conveniently can with one inhalation, provided the phrase permits it.

TECHNICAL MATERIAL

"I give many vocalises and exercises, which I invent to fit the needs of each pupil. I do not require them to be written down, simply remembered.

At the next lesson quite a different set of exercises may be recommended. I also make exercises out of familiar tunes or themes from operatic airs. It will be found that technical material in the various manuals is often chosen from such sources, so why not use them in their original form. Thus while the student is studying technic he is also acquiring much beautiful material, which will be of great value to him later on.

THE STUDY OF REPERTOIRE

"Repertoire is a wide subject and offers a fascinating study to the vocal student. He must have both imagination and sentiment, also the ability to portray, through movement and facial expression, the various moods and states of feeling indicated by words and music.

"In taking up a new role, I read the story to get at the kernel or plot, and see what it means. The composer first saw the words of a poem or libretto, and these suggested to him suitable music. So the singer begins his work by carefully reading the words.

"I then have the music of the whole work played for me on the piano, so as to discover its trend and meaning—its content. If the composer is available I ask him to do this. I next begin to study my own part in detail, not only the important sections but the little bits, which seem so small, but are often so difficult to remember."

CHARACTERIZATION

Under this head the singer spoke at length of the difficulty some singers encounter when they endeavor to portray character, or differentiate emotions. There is endless scope in this line, to exercise intelligence and imagination.

"Some singers," continued the artist, "seem incapable of characterizing a role or song. They can do what I call 'flat work', but cannot individualize a role. A singer may have a beautiful voice yet not be temperamental; he may have no gift for acting, nor be able to do character work.

"At the present moment I am preparing several new roles, three of them are of old men. It rests with me to externalize these three in such a way that they shall all be different, yet consistent with the characters as I understand them. Each make-up must be distinctive, and my work is to portray the parts as I see and feel them. I must get into the skin of each character, so to say, then act as I conceive that particular person would behave under like circumstances. Many singers cannot act, and most actors cannot sing. When the two are combined we have a singing actor, or an actor-singer. Once there was a popular belief that it was not necessary for the singer to know much about acting—if he only had a voice and could sing.

The present is changing all that. Many of us realize how very much study is required to perfect this side of our art.

"In this connection I am reminded of my London debut. I was to make it with the Royal English Opera Company. They heard me three times before deciding to take me on. With this formality over, rehearsals began. I soon found that my ideas of how my role—an important one—was to be acted, did not always coincide with the views of the stage director, and there were ructions. The manager saw how things were going, and advised me to accept seemingly the ideas of the stage director during rehearsals, but to study acting with the highest authorities and then work out the conception after my own ideas. Accordingly, I spent an hour daily, before the morning rehearsal, with one of the finest actors of comedy to be found in London. Later in the day, after rehearsal, I spent another hour with a great tragic actor. Thus I worked in both lines, as my part was a mixture of the tragic and the comic. I put in several weeks of very hard work in this way, and felt I had gained greatly. Of course this was entirely on the histrionic side, but it gives an idea of the preparation one needs.

"When the day of the dress rehearsal arrived, I appeared on the scene in full regalia, clean shaven (I had been wearing a beard until then), and performed my role as I had conceived it, regardless of the peculiar ideas of the stage director. At the first performance I made a hit, and a little later was engaged for grand opera at Covent Garden, where I remained for ten years.

KNOWLEDGE OF ANATOMY

"While I believe in understanding one's anatomy sufficiently for proper tone production, and all that goes with it, there are many peculiar and unnecessary fads and tricks resorted to by those who call themselves teachers of singing. The more fantastic the theories inculcated by these people, the more the unwary students seem to believe in them. People like to be deluded, you know. But I am not able to gratify their desires in this direction; for I can't lie about music!

"I was present at a vocal lesson given by one of these so-called instructors. 'You must sing in such a way that the tone will seem to come out of the back of your head', he told the pupil, and he waved his arms about his head as though he were drawing the tone out visibly. Another pupil was placed flat on his back, then told to breathe as though he were asleep, and then had to sing in that position. Another teacher I know of makes pupils eject spit-balls of tissue paper at the ceiling, to learn the alleged proper control of the breath. What criminal nonsense this is!

"As I have said, I believe in knowing what is necessary about anatomy, but not in too great measure. A new book will soon be issued, I am told, which actually dissects the human body, showing every bone and muscle in any way connected with breath or voice. All this may be of interest as a matter of research, but must one go into such minutiæ in order to teach singing? I think the answer must ever be in the negative. You might as well talk to a gold-fish in a bowl and say: 'If you desire to proceed laterally to the right, kindly oscillate gently your sinister dorsal fin, and you will achieve the desired result.' Oh, Art, what sins are committed in thy name!"

IN THE STUDIO

It is often affirmed that an artist finds experience the best teacher. It must be equally true that the artist-teacher of wide experience in both performance and instruction, should be a safe guide, just because of this varied experience.

I was impressed with this fact when I recently had the privilege of visiting Mr. Bispham's studio during lesson hours, and listening to his instruction. A most interesting sanctum is this studio, filled as it is with souvenirs and pictures of the artist's long career on the operatic stage. Here hangs a drawing in color of Bispham as Telramund, in shining chain armor; there a life-size portrait as "Beethoven," and again as himself. In the midst of all is the master, seated at a table. In front of him, at the piano, stands the student. It is an English song she is at work on, for Mr. Bispham thoroughly believes in mastering English as well as other languages.

How alert he is as he sits there; how keen of eye and ear. Not the slightest fault escapes him. He often sings the phrase himself, then calls for its repetition.

"Sing that passage again; there is a tone in it that is not pleasant—not well-sounding; make it beautiful!" "Careful of your consonants there, they are not distinct; let them be clearer, but don't make them over-distinct." "Don't scoop up the ends of the phrases; make the tones this way"; and he illustrates repeatedly. "Sing this phrase in one breath if you can, if not, breathe here—" indicating the place.

The student now takes up an Italian aria. Of course the master teacher has no need of printed score; he knows the arias by heart. He merely jots down a few remarks on a slip of paper, to be referred to later.

The aria goes quite well. At its close the singer goes to her seat and another takes her place. A voice of rich, warm timbre. More English—and it must be most exact, to suit Mr. Bispham's fastidious ear.

"Make the word *fire* in *one* syllable, not *two*. Do not open the mouth quite so wide on the word *desire*, for, by doing so you lose the balance and the tone is not so good."

VOCALISES

Another student—with a fine tenor—was asked to vocalize for a number of minutes. He sang ascending and descending tone-figures, sometimes doing them in one breath, at others taking a fresh breath at top. Some of the syllables used were: "la," "ma," "may," and "mi." He then sang single tones, swelling and diminishing each. It was found that passing from *forte* to *piano* was much more difficult than swelling from soft to loud.

The aria "Be not afraid" was now taken up; it was pronounced one of the most difficult solos ever written, and a very valuable composition for vocal training.

"You sing that phrase too loud," cautioned the instructor. "This is not a human being who is speaking, rather it is a heavenly voice. That high note of the phrase should be made softer, more ethereal. Make it a *young tone*—put the quality of Spring into it. The whole thing should be more spiritual or spiritualized. Now go through it again from beginning to end."

When this was finished a halt was called; there had been enough work done for that day. Soon the class was dismissed. The young singers—some if not all of them known upon the concert stage—filed out. One young woman remained; she was to have a drama lesson. The master of singing showed himself equally efficient as master of English diction for the spoken drama.

And here, for a time, we must leave him at his work.

෴

Making a Career in America

An interview with
SOPHIE BRASLAU

by Harriette Brower

A fact often overlooked when considering the career of some of our great singers of today is that they started out to become an instrumentalist rather than a singer. In other words they become proficient on some instrument before taking up serious study of the voice. In this connection one thinks of Mme. Sembrich, who was both pianist and violinist before becoming known as a singer. It would be interesting to follow up this idea and enumerate the vocalists who have broadened their musicianship through the study of other instruments than their own voices. But this delightful task must be reserved for future leisure. For the present it can be set down here that Miss Sophie Braslau, probably the youngest star in the constellation of the Metropolitan artists, is an accomplished pianist, and intended to make her career with the aid of that instrument instead of with her voice.

But we will let the young artist speak for herself. On the occasion in question, she had just returned from a walk, her arms full of rosebuds. "I never can resist flowers," she remarked, as she had them placed in a big silver vase. Then she carried the visitor off to her own special rooms, whose windows overlooked an inner garden, where one forgot one was in the heart of New York. "Indeed it is not like New York at all, rather like Paris," said Miss Braslau, answering my thought.

On a *chaise longue* in this ivory and rose sanctum, reposed a big, beautiful doll, preserved from childish days. The singer took it up; "I don't play with it now," she said with a smile, "but I used to." She placed it carefully in a chair, then settled herself to talk.

"Yes, I intended to make the piano my instrument and began my studies at the age of six. Before long it was seen that I had something of a voice, but no one gave it much thought, supposing I was to be a pianist; indeed I have the hand of one," holding it up. "I don't think, in those early years, I was so very anxious to become a player. I did not love scales—do not now, and would quite as soon have sat at the piano with a book in my lap, while my fingers mechanically did their stunts. But my mother looked after my practice, and often sat near me. She required a regular amount of time given to music study each day. I am so grateful that she was strict with me, for my knowledge of piano and its literature is the greatest joy to me now. To my thinking all children should have piano lessons; the cost is trifling compared to the benefits they receive. They should be made to study, whether they wish to or not. They are not prepared to judge what is good for them, and if they are given this advantage they will be glad of it later on.

"In due time I entered the Institute of Musical Art, taking the full piano course. Arthur Hochmann was my teacher for piano, and I found him an excellent master. He did a great deal for me; in interpretation, in fineness of detail, in artistic finish I owe him very much. Later I studied several years with Alexander Lambert.

"While at work with my piano, it grew more apparent that I had a voice that should be cultivated. So I began. Afterwards I worked three years with Signor Buzzi Peccia, who started me on an operatic career and finally brought me to the Metropolitan.

"It was a great ordeal for a young singer, almost a beginner, to start at our greatest Opera House! It meant unremitting labor for me. I worked very hard, but I am not afraid of work. Toscanini held sway when I began, and he was a marvelous musician and conductor. Such exactness, such perfection of detail; he required perfection of everyone. He did not at first realize how much of a beginner I was, though I had really learned a large number of roles. He was so strict in every detail that I wept many bitter tears for fear I would not come up to the mark. I knew the music, but had not gained experience through routine. It seems to me every singer should gain this experience in some smaller places before attempting the highest. My advice would be to go and get experience in Europe first. I have never been in Germany, but in Italy and France there are many small opera houses where one may learn routine.

"Another thing. There is a mistaken notion that one cannot reach any height in opera without 'pull' and great influence. I am sure this is not true; for while a pull may help, one must be able to deliver the goods. If one cannot, all the backing in the world will not make one a success. The singer must have the ability to 'put it over'. Think of the artists who can do it— Farrar, Gluck, Schumann-Heink. There is never any doubt about them; they always win their audiences. What I have done has been accomplished by hard work, without backing of any kind. Really of what use is backing anyway? The public can judge—or at least it can *feel*. I know very well that when my chance came to sing *Shanewis,** if I had not been able to do it, no amount of influence would have helped the situation. I had it in my own hand to make or mar my career. I often wonder whether audiences really know anything about what you are trying to do; whether they have any conception of what is right in singing, or whether they are merely swayed by the temperament of the singer.

"Whether we are or are not to be a musical nation should be a question of deep interest to all music lovers. If we really become a great musical people, it will be largely due to the work of the records. We certainly have wonderful advantages here, and are doing a tremendous lot for music.

"I had an interesting experience recently. It was in a little town in North Carolina, where a song recital had never before been given. Can you fancy a place where there had never even been a concert? The people in this little town were busy producing tobacco and had never turned their thought toward music. In the face of the coming concert what did those people do?

[*a two-act opera by Charles Wakefield Cadman, first performed at the Metropolitan Opera, March 1918]

They got a program, studied what pieces I had sung on the Victor, got the music of the others; so they had a pretty good idea of what I was going to sing. When I stepped on the platform that night and saw the little upright piano (no other instrument could be secured) and looked into those eager faces, I wondered how they would receive my work. My first number was an aria from *Orfeo*. When I finished, the demonstration was so deafening I had to wait minutes before I could go on. And so it continued all the evening.

"How do I work? Very hard, at least six hours a day. Of these I actually sing perhaps three hours. I begin at nine and give the first hour to memory work on repertoire. I give very thorough study to my programs; for I must know every note in them, both for voice and piano. I make it a point to know the accompaniments, for in case I am ever left without an accompanist, I can play for myself, and it has a great effect on audiences. They may not know or care whether you can play Beethoven or Chopin, but the fact that you can play while you sing greatly impresses them.

"In committing a song, I play it over and sing it sufficiently to get a good idea of its construction and meaning; then I work in detail, learning words and music at the same time, usually. Certain things are very difficult for me, things requiring absolute evenness of passage work, or sustained calm. Naturally I have an excess of temperament; I feel things in a vivid, passionate way. So I need to go very slowly at times. To-day I gave several hours to only three lines of an aria by Haendel, and am not yet satisfied with it. Indeed, can we ever rest satisfied, when there is so much to learn, and we can always improve?

"The second hour of my day is given to vocalises. Of course there are certain standard things that one must do; but there are others that need not be done every day. I try to vary the work as much as I can.

"The rest of the day is given to study on repertoire and all the things that belong to it. There is so much more to a singer's art than merely to sing. And it is a sad thing to find that so many singers lack musicianship. They seem to think if they can sing some songs, or even a few operas, that is all there is to it. But one who would become an artist must work most of the time. I am sure Charles Hackett knows the value of work; so does Mabel Garrison and many other Americans. And when you think of it, there are really a brave number of our own singers who are not only making good, but making big names for themselves and winning the success that comes from a union of talent and industry."

Success in Concert Singing

by

Dame Clara Butt

[Biographical sketch by James Francis Cooke]

[Dame Butt was born at Southwick, Sussex, February 1, 1873. Her first lessons were with D. W. Rootham in Bristol.

In 1889 she won a scholarship at the Royal College of Music where the teacher was J. H. Blower. Later she studied for short periods with Bouhy in Paris and Etelka Gerster in Berlin. Her debut was made as Ursula in Sullivan's setting of the Longfellow poem *Golden Legend*. Her success was immediate and very great. She became in demand at all of the great English musical festivals and also sang before enormous audiences for years in the great English cities. In 1900 she married the noted English baritone R. Kennerly Rumford and together they have made many tours, including a tour of the world, appearing everywhere with continued success. Her voice is one of rich, full contralto quality with such individual characteristics that great English composers have written special works to reveal these great natural gifts. Dame Butt received her distinction of "Dame" from King George in 1920. Her happy family life with her children has won her endless admirers among musical people everywhere.]

Health and Singing

It must be obvious to all aspiring vocal students that splendid good health is well nigh indispensable to the singer. There have been singers, of course, who have had physical afflictions that have made their public appearances extremely painful, but they have succeeded in spite of these unfortunate drawbacks. In fact, if the younger singer is ambitious and has that wonderful gift of directing her efforts in the way most likely to bring fortunate results, even physical weakness may be overcome. By this I mean that the singer will work out some plan for bringing her physical condition to the standard that fine singing demands. I believe most emphatically that the right spirit will conquer obstacles that often seem impassable. One might safely say that nine-tenths of the successes in all branches of artistic work are due to the inextinguishable fire that burns in the heart and mind of the art worker and incites him to pass through any ordeal in order to deliver his message to the world.

MISDIRECTED EFFORT

The cruel part of it all is that many aspire to become great singers who can never possibly have their hopes realized. Natural selection rather than destiny seems to govern this matter. The ugly caterpillar seems like an unpromising candidate for the brilliant career of the butterfly, and it oftentimes happens that students who seem unpromising to some have just the qualities which, with the right time, instruction and experience, will entitle them to great success. It is the little ant who hopes to grow iridescent wings, and who travels through conservatory after conservatory, hoping to find the magic chrysalis that will do this, who is to be pitied. Great success must depend upon special gifts, intellectual as well as vocal. Oh, if we only had some instinct, like that possessed by animals, that would enable us to determine accurately in advance the safest road for us to take, the road that will lead us to the best development of our real talents—not those we imagine we may have or those which the flattery of friends have grafted upon us! Mr. Rumford and I have witnessed so much very hard and very earnest work carried on by students who have no rational basis to hope for success as singers, that we have been placed in the uncomfortable position of advising young singers to seek some other life work.

WHEN TO BEGIN

The eternal question, "At what age shall I commence to study singing?" is always more or less amusing to the experienced singer. If the singer's spirit is in the child, nothing will stop his singing. He will sing from morning until night, and seems to be guided in most cases by an all-providing Nature that makes its untutored efforts the very best kind of practice. Unless the child is brought into contact with very bad music he is not likely to be injured. Children seem to be trying their best to prove the Darwinian theory by showing us that they can mimic quite as well as monkeys. The average child comes into the better part of his little store of wisdom through mimicry. Naturally if the little vocal student is taken to the vaudeville theatre, where every imaginable vocal law is smashed during a three-hour performance, and if the child observes that the smashing process is followed by the enthusiastic applause of the unthinking audience, it is only reasonable to suppose that the child will discover in this what he believes to be the most approved art of singing.

It is evident then that the first thing which the parent of the musical child should consider is that of teaching him to appreciate what is looked upon as good and what is looked upon as bad. Although many singers with fine voices have appeared in vaudeville, the others must be regarded as "horrible" examples, and the child should know that they are such. On the other hand, it is quite evident that the more good singing that the child hears in the impressionable years of its youth the greater will be the effect upon the mind which is to direct the child's musical future. This is a branch of the vocalist's education which may begin long before the actual lessons. If it is carefully conducted the teacher should have far less difficulty in starting the child with the actual work. The only possible danger might be that the child's imitative faculty could lead it to extremes of pitch in imitating some singer. Even this is hardly more likely to injure it than the shouting and screaming which often accompanies the play of children.

The actual time of starting must depend upon the individual. It is never too early for him to start in acquiring his musical knowledge. Everything he might learn of music itself, through the study of the piano or any other instrument would all become a part of his capital when he became a singer. Those singers are fortunate whose musical knowledge commenced with the cradle and whose first master was that greatest of all teachers, the mother. Speaking generally, it seems to be the impression of singing teachers that voice students should not commence the vocal side of their studies until they are from sixteen to seventeen years of age. In this connection, consider my own case. My first public appearance with orchestra was when I was fourteen. It was in Bristol, England, and among other things I sang "Ora Pro Nobis" from Gounod's *Workers.**

I was fortunate in having in my first teacher, D. W. Rootham, a man too thoroughly blessed with good British common sense to have any "tricks." He had no fantastic way of doing things, no proprietary methods, that none else in the world was supposed to possess. He listened for the beautiful in my voice and, as his sense of musical appreciation was highly cultivated, he could detect faults, explain them to me and show me how to overcome them by purely natural methods. The principal part of the process was to make me realize mentally just what was wrong and then what was the more artistic way of doing it.

LETTING THE VOICE GROW

After all, singing is singing, and I am convinced that my master's idea of just letting the voice grow with normal exercise and without excesses in any direction was the best way for me. It was certainly better than hours and hours of theory, interesting to the student of physiology, but often bewildering to the young vocalist. Real singing with real music is immeasurably better than ages of conjecture. It appears that some students spend years in learning how they are going to sing at some glorious day in the future, but it never seems to occur to them that in order to sing they must really

[*presumably "The Worker," a secular song to a text by F. Weatherly, orchestrated by the composer]

use their voices. Of course, I do not mean to infer that the student must omit the necessary preparatory work. Solfeggios, for instance, and scales are extremely useful. Concone, tried and true, gives excellent material for all students. But why spend years of dreaming of theories regarding singing when everyone knows that the theory of singing has been the battleground for innumerable talented writers for centuries? Even now it is apparently impossible to reconcile all the vocal writers, except in so far as they all modestly admit that they have rediscovered the real old Italian school. Perhaps they have. But, admitting that an art teacher rediscovered the actual pigments used by Leonardo da Vinci, Rembrandt or Raphael, he would have no little task in creating a student who could duplicate *Mona Lisa, The Night Watch* or the *Sistine Madonna.*

After leaving Rootham, I won the four-hundred-guinea scholarship at the Royal College of Music and studied with Henry Blower. This I followed with a course with Bouhy in Paris and Etelka Gerster in Berlin. Mr. Rumford and I both concur in the opinion that it is necessary for the student who would sing in any foreign language to study in the country in which the language is spoken. In no other way can one get the real atmosphere. The preparatory work may be done in the home country, but if one fails to taste of the musical life of the country in which the songs came into being, there seems to be an indefinable absence of the right flavor. I believe in employing the native tongue for songs in recital work. It seems narrow to me to do otherwise. At the same time, I have always been a champion for songs written originally with English texts, and have sung innumerable times with programs made from English lyrics.

Preparing a Repertoire

The idea that concert and recital work is not as difficult as operatic work has been pretty well exploded by this time. In fact, it is very much more difficult to sing a simple song well in concert than it is to sing some of the elaborate Wagnerian recitatives in which the very complexities of the music make a convenient hiding place for the artist's vocal shortcomings. In concert everything is concentrated upon the singer. Convention has ever deprived him of the convenient gestures that give ease to the opera singer.

The selection of useful material for concert purposes is immensely difficult. It must have artistic merit, it must have human interest, it must suit the singer, in most cases the piano must be used for accompaniment and the song must not be dependent upon an orchestral accompaniment for its value. It must not be too old, it must not be too far in advance of popular tastes. It is a bad plan to wander indiscriminately about among countless songs, never learning any really well. The student should begin to select numbers with great care, realizing that it is futile to try to do every-thing. Lord Bolingbroke, in his essay on the shortness of human life, shows how impossible it is for a man to read more than a mere fraction of a great library though he read regularly every day of his life. It is very much the same with music. The resources are so vast and time is so limited that there is no opportunity to learn everything. Far better is it for the vocalist to do a little well than to do much ineffectually.

Good music well executed meets with very much the same appreciation everywhere. During our latest tour we gave almost the very same programs in America as those we have been giving upon the European Continent. The music-loving American public is likely to differ but slightly from that of the great music centers of the old world. Music has truly become a uni-versal language.

In developing a repertoire the student might look upon the musical pub-lic as though it were a huge circle filled with smaller circles, each little cir-cle being a center of interest. One circle might insist upon old English songs, such as the delightful melodies of Arne, Carey, Monroe. Another circle might expect the arias of the old Italian masters, Carissimi, Jomelli, Sacchini or Scarlatti. Another circle would want to hear the German Lieder of such composers as Schumann, Schubert, Brahms, Franz and Wolf. Still another circle might go away disappointed if they could not hear something of the ultra-modern writers, such as Strauss, Debussy or even that freak of musi-cal cacophony, Schoenberg. However diverse may be the individual likings of these smaller circles, all of the members of your audience are united in liking music as a whole.

The audience will demand variety in your repertoire but at the same time it will demand certain musical essentials which appeal to all. There is one circle in your audience that I have purposely reserved for separate discus-sion. That is the great circle of concert goers who are not skilled musicians, who are too frank, too candid, to adopt any of the cant of those social frauds who revel in Reger and Schoenberg, and just because it might stamp them as real connoisseurs, but who really can't recognize much difference between the "Liebestod" of *Tristan und Isolde* and "Rule Britannia"—but the music lovers who are too honest to fail to state that they like "The Lost Chord" or the lovely folk songs of your American composer Stephen Foster. Mr. Plunkett Greene, in his work upon song interpretation, makes no room for the existence of songs of this kind. Indeed, he would cast them all into the discard. This seems to me a huge mistake. Surely we can not say that music is a monopoly of the few who have schooled their ears to enjoy out-landish dissonances with delight. Music is perhaps the most universal of all the arts and with the gradual evolution of those who love it, a natural au-dience is provided for music of the more complicated sort. We learn to like our musical caviar with surprising rapidity. It was only yesterday that we were objecting to the delightful piano pieces of Debussy, who can generate an atmosphere with a single chord just as Murillo could inspire an emotion with a stroke of the brush.

It is not safe to say that you do not like things in this way. I think that even Schoenberg is trying to be true to his muse. We must remember that Haydn, Beethoven, Wagner and Brahms passed through the fire of criticism in their day. The more breadth a singer puts into her work the more likely is she to reap success. Time only can produce the accomplished artist. The best is to find a joy in your work and think of nothing but large success. If you have the gift, triumph will be yours.

❧

Italy, the Home of Song

by

ENRICO CARUSO

[Biographical sketch by James Francis Cooke]

[Enrico Caruso was born in Naples, February 25th, 1873. His fondness for music dates from his earliest childhood; and he spent much of his spare money in attending the opera at San Carlo and hearing the foremost singers of his time in many of the roles in which he appeared later on. His actual study, however, did not start until he was eighteen, when he came under the tuition of Guglielmo Vergine. In 1895 he made his debut at the Teatro Cimarosa in Caserta. His first appearances drew comparatively little attention to his work and his future greatness was hardly suspected by many of those who heard him. However, by dint of long application to his art he gained more and more recognition. In 1902 he made his debut in London. The following year he came to New York, where the world's greatest singers had found an El Dorado for nearly a quarter of a century. There he was at once proclaimed the greatest of all tenors and from that time his success was undeviating. Indeed his voice was so wonderful and so individual that it is difficult to compare him with any of his great predecessors: Tamagno, Campanini, de Reszke and others. In Europe and in America he was welcomed with acclaim and the records of his voice are to be found in thousands of homes of music lovers who have never come in touch with him in any other way. Signor Caruso had a remarkable talent for drawing and for sculpture. His death, August 2d, 1921, ended the career of the greatest male singer of history.]

OPERA AND THE PUBLIC IN ITALY

Anyone who has traveled in Italy must have noticed the interest that is manifested at the opening of the opera season. This does not apply only to the people with means and advanced culture but also to what might be called the general public. In addition to the upper classes, the same class of people in America who would show the wildest enthusiasm over your popular sport, base-ball, would be similarly eager to attend the leading operatic performances in Italy. The opening of the opera is accompanied by an indescribable fervor. It is "in the air." The whole community seems to breathe opera. The children know the leading melodies, and often discuss the features of the performances as they hear their parents tell about them, just as the American small boy retails his father's opinions upon the political struggles of the day or upon the last ball game.

It should not be thought that this does not mean a sacrifice to the masses, for opera is, in a sense, more expensive in Italy than in America; that is, it is more expensive by comparison in most parts of the country. It should be remembered that monetary values in Italy are entirely different from those in America. The average Italian of moderate means looks upon a lira as a coin far more valuable than its equivalent of twenty cents in United States currency. His income is likely to be limited, and he must spend it with care and wisdom. Again, in the great operatic centers, such as Milan, Naples or Rome, the prices are invariably adjusted to the importance of the production. In first-class productions the prices are often very high from the Italian standpoint. For instance, at La Scala in Milan, when an exceptionally fine performance is given with really great singers, the prices for orchestra chairs may run as high as thirty lira or six dollars a seat. Even to the wealthy Italian this amount seems the same as a much larger amount in America.

To give opera in Italy with the same spectacular effects, the same casts composed almost exclusively of very renowned artists, the same *mise en scène,* etc., would require a price of admission really higher than in America. As a matter of fact, there is no place in the world where such a great number of performances, with so many world-renowned singers, are given as at the Metropolitan Opera House in New York. There is no necessity for any one to make a special trip to Europe to hear excellent performances in these days. Of course such a trip would be interesting, as the performances given in many European centers are wonderfully fine, and they would be interesting to hear if only from the standpoint of comparing them with those given at the Metropolitan. However, the most eminent singers of the world come here constantly, and the performances are directed by the ablest men obtainable, and I am at loss to see why America should not be extremely proud of her operatic advantages. In addition to this the public manifests a most intelligent appreciation of the best in music. It is very agreeable to sing in America, as one is sure that when he does well the public will respond at once.

ITALIAN, THE LANGUAGE OF MUSIC

Perhaps the fact that in Italy the audiences may understand the performances better because of their knowledge of their native language may add to the pleasure of opera-going. This, however, is a question, except in the case of some of the more modern works. The older opera librettos left much to be desired from the dramatic and poetic standpoints. Italian after all is the language of music. In fact it is music in itself when properly spoken. Note that I say "when properly spoken." American girls go to Italy to study, and of course desire to acquire a knowledge of the language itself, for they have heard that it is beneficial in singing. They get a mere smattering, and do not make any attempt to secure a perfect accent. The result is about as funny as the efforts of the comedians who imitate German emigrants on the American stage.

If you start the study of Italian, persist until you have really mastered the language. In doing this your ear will get such a drill and such a series of exercises as it has never had before. You will have to listen to the vowel sounds as you have never listened. This is necessary because in order to understand the grammar of the language you must hear the final vowel in each word and you must hear the consonants distinctly.

There is another peculiar thing about Italian. If the student who has always studied and sung in English, German or French or Russian, attempts to sing in Italian, he is really turning a brilliant searchlight upon his own vocal ability. If he has any faults which have been concealed in his singing in his own language, they will be discovered at once the moment he commences to study in Italian. I do not know whether this is because the Italian of culture has a higher standard of diction in the enunciation of the vowel sounds, or whether the sounds themselves are so pure and smooth that they expose the deficiencies, but it is nevertheless the case. The American girl who studies Italian for six months and then hopes to sing in that language in a manner not likely to disturb the sense of the ridiculous is deceiving herself. It takes years to acquire fluency in a language.

AUDIENCES THE SAME THE WORLD AROUND

Audiences are as sensitive as individuals. Italy is known as "the home of the opera"; but I find that, as far as manifesting enthusiasm goes, the world is getting pretty much the same. If the public is pleased, it applauds no matter whether it be in Vienna, Paris, Rome, Buenos Aires, New York, or

Oshkosh. An artist feels his bond with his audience very quickly. He knows whether his auditors are delighted, whether they are merely interested or whether they are indifferent a few seconds after he has been upon the stage. I can judge my own work at once by the attitude of the audience. No artist sings exactly alike on two successive nights. That would be impossible. Although every sincere artist tries to do his best at all times, there are, nevertheless, occasions when one sings better than at others. If I sing particularly well the audience is particularly enthusiastic; if I am not feeling well and my singing indicates it, the audience will let me know at once by not being quite so enthusiastic. It is a barometer which is almost unfailing. This is also an important thing for the young singer to consider. Audiences judge by real worth and not by reputation.

Reputation may attract money to the box office, but once the people are inside the opera house the artist must really please them or suffer. Young singers should not be led to think that anything but real worth is of any lasting value. If the audience does not respond, do not blame the audience. It would respond if you could sing so beautifully that you could compel a response that you know should follow real artistic achievement. Don't blame your teacher or your lack of practice or anything or anybody but yourself. The verdict of the audience is better than the examination of a hundred so-called experts. There is something about an audience that makes it seem like a great human individual, whether in Naples or in San Francisco. If you touch the heart or please the sense of beauty, the appetite for lovely music—common to all mankind—the audience is yours, be it Italian, French, German or American.

OPERATIC PREPARATION IN ITALY

The American student with a really good voice and a really fine vocal and musical training, would have more opportunities for engagements in the smaller Italian opera houses, for the simple reason that there are more of these opera houses and more of these opera companies. Bear in mind, however, that opera in Italy depends to a large extent upon the standing of the artists engaged to put on the opera. In some cities of the smaller size the municipality makes an appropriation, which serves as a guarantee or subsidy. An impresario is informed what operas the community desires and what singers. He tries to comply with the demand. Often the city is very small and the demand very slightly indicated in real money. As a result the performances are comparatively mediocre. The American student sometimes fails to secure engagements with the big companies and tries to gain experience in these small companies. Sometimes he succeeds, but he should remember before undertaking this work that many native Italian singers with really fine voices are looking for similar opportunities and that only a very few stand any chance of reaching really noteworthy success.

OPERA WILL ALWAYS BE EXPENSIVE

He should, of course, endeavor to seek engagements with the big companies if his voice and ability will warrant it. Where the most money is, there will be the salaried artists and the finest operatic spectacle. That is axiomatic. Opera is expensive and will always be expensive. The supply of unusual voices has always been limited and the services of their possessors have always commanded a high reward. This is based upon an economic law which applies to all things in life. The young singer should realize that, unless he can rise to the very top of his profession, he will be compelled to enlist in a veritable army of singers with little talent and less opportunity.

One thing exists in Italy which is very greatly missed in America. Even in small companies in Italy a great deal of time is spent in rehearsals. In America rehearsals are tremendously expensive and sometimes first performances have suffered thereby. In fact, I doubt whether the public realizes what a very expensive thing opera is. The public has little opportunity to look behind the scenes. It sees only the finished performance, which runs smoothly only when a tremendous amount of mental, physical and financial oil has been poured upon the machinery. I often hear men say here in New York, "I had to pay fifty dollars for my seat to-night." That is absurd—the money is going to speculators instead of into the rightful channels. This money is simply lost as far as doing any service whatever to art is concerned. It does not go into the opera house treasury to make for better performances, but simply into the hands of some fellow who had been clever enough to deprive the public of its just opportunity to purchase seats. The public seems to have money enough to pay an outrageous amount for seats when necessary. Would it not be better to do away with the speculator at the door and pay, say, $10.00 for a seat that now costs $7.00? This would mean more rehearsals and better opera and no money donated to the undeserving horde at the portals of the temple.

THE STUDENT'S PREPARATION

I am told that many people in America have the impression that my vocal ability is kind of a "God-given" gift; that is, something that has come to me without effort. This is so very absurd that I can hardly believe that sensible people would give it a moment's credence. Every voice is in a sense the result of a development, and this is particularly so in my own case. The marble that comes from the quarries of Carrara may be very beautiful and white and flawless, but it does not shape itself into a work of art without the hand, the heart, and the intellect of the sculptor.

Just to show how utterly ridiculous this popular opinion really is, let me cite the fact that at the age of fifteen everybody who heard me sing pronounced me a bass. When I went to Vergine I studied hard for four years. During the first three years the work was for the most part moulding and shaping the voice. Then I studied repertoire for one year and made my de-, but. Even with the experience I had had at that time it was unreasonable to expect great success at once. I kept working hard and worked for at least seven years more before any really mentionable success came to me. All the time I had one thing on my mind and that was never to let a day pass without seeing some improvement in my voice. The discouragements were frequent and bitter; but I kept on working and waiting until my long awaited opportunities came in London and in New York. The great thing is, not to stop. Do not think that, because these great cities gave me a flattering reception, my work ceased. Quite on the contrary, I kept on working and am working still. Every time I go upon the stage I am endeavoring to discover something that will make my art more worthy of public acceptance. Every act of each opera is a new lesson.

DIFFERENT ROLES

It is difficult to invest a role with individuality. I have no favorite roles. I have avoided this, because the moment one adopts a favorite role he becomes a specialist and ceases to be an artist. The artist does all roles equally well. I have had the unique experience of creating many roles in operas such as *Fedora, Adrienne, Germania, Girl of the Golden West, Maschera*. This is a splendid experience, as it always taxes the inventive faculties of the singing actor. This is particularly the case in the Italian opera of the newer composers, or rather the composers who have worked in Italy since the reformation of Wagner. Whatever may be said, the greatest influence in modern Italian opera is Wagner. Even the great Verdi was induced to change his methods in *Aïda, Otello,* and *Falstaff*—all representing a much higher art than his earlier operas. However, Wagner did nothing to rob Italy of its natural gift of melody, even though he did institute a reform. He also did not influence such modern composers as Puccini, Mascagni, and Leoncavallo to the extent of marring their native originality and fertility.

Modern Roads to Vocal Success

by

JULIA CLAUSSEN

[Biographical sketch by James Francis Cooke]

[Mme. Julia Claussen was born at Stockholm, Sweden, the land of Jenny Lind and Nilsson. Her voice is a rich, flexible mezzo-soprano, with a range that has enabled her to assume some contralto roles with more success than the average so-called contralto. In her childhood she studied piano, but did not undertake the serious study of voice until she was eighteen, when she became a student at the Royal Academy of Music, under Professor Lejdstrom (studying harmony and theory under the famous Swedish composer Sjögren). Her debut was made at the Royal Opera, at the age of twenty-two, in *La Favorita,* singing the role in Swedish. Later she went to Berlin, where she was coached in German opera by Professor Friedrich at the Royal High School of Music. Her American debut was made in 1912, in Chicago, where she made an immediate success in such roles as Ortrud, Brünnhilde and Carmen. She was then engaged at Covent Garden and later sang at the Champs-Elysées Theatre, under Nikisch, in Paris. For two years she appeared at the Metropolitan. She has received the rare distinction of being awarded the Jenny Lind Medal from her own government and also of being admitted to the Royal Academy of Sweden, the youngest member ever elected to that august scientific and artistic body. She has also been decorated by King Gustavus V of Sweden with *Literis et Artibus*. In America she has made an immense success as a concert singer.]

WHY SWEDEN PRODUCES SO MANY SINGERS

The question, "Why does Sweden produce so many singers?" is often asked me. First it is a matter of climate, then a matter of physique, and lastly, because the Swedish children do far more singing than any one finds in many other countries. The air in Sweden is very rarefied, clear and exhilarating. Owing to frugal living and abundant systematic exercise, the people become very robust. This is not a matter of one generation or so, but goes back for centuries. The Swedes are a strong, energetic, thorough race; and the same attributes of industry and precision which have made them famous in science are applied to the study of music.

The Swedish child is made to understand that singing is a needful, serious part of his life. His musical training begins very early in the schools, with a definite scheme. All schools have competent, experienced teachers of singing. In my childhood another factor played a very important part. There was never the endless round of attractions, toys, parties, theatres and pastimes (to say nothing of the all-consuming movies). Life was more tranquil and therefore the pursuit of good music was far more enjoyable. American life moves at aeroplane speed. The poor little children hardly have time to breathe, let alone time to study music. Ragtime is the musical symptom of this American craving for speed and incessant excitement. In a blare and confusion of noises, like bedlam broken loose, what chance has a child to develop good taste? It is admittedly fascinating at times; but is without rhyme, reason or order. I never permit my children to pollute my piano with it. They may have it on the talking machine, but they must not be accomplices in making it.

Of course, things have changed in Sweden, too; and American ragtime, always contagious, has now infected all Europe. This makes the music teacher's task in this day far more difficult than formerly. I hear my daughters practicing, and now and then they seem to be putting a dash of ragtime into Bach. If I stop them I find that "Bach is too slow, I don't like Bach!" This is almost like saying, "I don't like Rubens, Van Dyke or Millet; please, teacher, give me Mutt and Jeff or the Katzenjammer Kids!" American children need to be constantly taught to reverence the great creators of the land. Why, Jenny Lind is looked upon as a great national heroine in Sweden, much as one might regard George Washington in America. Before America can go about musical educational work properly, the teachers must inculcate this spirit, a proper appreciation of what is really beautiful, instead of a kind of wild, mob-like orgy of blare, bang, smash and shriek which so many have come to know as ragtime and jazz.

SELF-CRITICISM

If one should ask me what is the first consideration in becoming a success as a singer, I should say the ability to criticise one's self. In my own case I had a very competent musician as a teacher. He told me that my voice was naturally placed and did very little to help place it according to his own ideas. Perhaps that was well for me, because I knew myself what I was about. He used to say, "That sounds beautiful," but all the time I knew that it sounded terrible. It was then that I learned that my ear must be my best teacher. My teacher, for instance, told me that I would never be able to trill. This was very disheartening; but he really believed, according to his conservative knowledge, that I should never succeed in getting the necessary flexibility.

By chance I happened to meet a celebrated Swedish singer, Mme. Östberg, of the old school. I communicated to her the discouraging news that

I could never hope to trill. "Nonsense, my dear," she said, "someone told me that too, but I determined that I was going to learn. I did not know how to go about it exactly, but I knew that with the proper patience and willpower I would succeed. Therefore I worked up to three o'clock one morning, and before I went to bed I was able to trill."

I decided to take Mme. Östberg's advice, and I practiced for several days until I knew that I could trill, and then I went back to my teacher and showed him what I could do. He had to admit it was a good trill, and he couldn't understand how I had so successfully disproved his theories by accomplishing it. It was then that I learned that the singer can do almost anything within the limits of the voice, if one will only work hard enough. Work is the great producer, and there is no substitute for it. Do not think that I am ungrateful to my teacher. He gave me a splendid musical drilling in all the standard solfeggios, in which he was most precise; and in later years I said to him, "I am not grateful to you for making my voice, but because you did not spoil it."

After having sung a great deal and thought introspectively a great deal about the voice, one naturally begins to form a kind of philosophy regarding it. Of course, breathing exercises are the basis of all good singing methods, but it seems to me that singing teachers ask many of their pupils to do many queer impractical things in breathing, things that "don't work" when the singer is obliged to stand up before a big audience and make everyone hear without straining.

If I were to teach a young girl right at this moment I would simply ask her to take a deep breath and note the expansion at the waist just above the diaphragm. Then I would ask her to say as many words as possible upon that breath, at the same time having the muscles adjacent to the diaphragm to support the breath; that is, to sustain it and not collapse or try to push it up. The trick is to get the most tone, not with the most breath but with the least breath, and especially the very least possible strain at the throat, which must be kept in a floating, gossamer-like condition all the time. I see girls, who have been to expensive teachers, doing all sorts of wonderful calisthenics with the diaphragm, things that God certainly did not intend us to do in learning to speak and to sing.

Any attempt to draw in the front walls of the abdomen or the intercostal muscles during singing must put a kind of pneumatic pressure upon the breath stream, which is sure to constrict the throat. Therefore, in my own singing, I note the opposite effect. That is, there is rather a sensation of expansion instead of contraction during the process of expiration. This soon becomes very comfortable, relieves the throat of strain, relieves the tones of breathiness or all idea of forcing. There is none of the ugly heaving of the chest or shoulders; the body is in repose, and the singer has a firm grip upon the tone in the right way. The muscles of the front wall of the abdomen and the muscles between the lower ribs become very strong and equal to any strain, while the throat is free.

In the emission of the actual tone itself I would advise the sensation of inhaling at first. The beginner should blow out the tone. Usually instead of having a lovely floating character, with the impression of control, the tone starts with being forced, and it always remains so. The singer oversings and has nothing in reserve. When I am singing I feel as though the farther away from the throat, the deeper down I can control the breath stream, the better and freer the tone becomes. Furthermore, I can sing the long, difficult Wagnerian roles, with their tremendous demands upon the vocal organs, without the least sensation of fatigue. Some singers, after such performances, are "all in." No wonder they lose their voices when they should be in their prime.

For me the most difficult vowel is "ah." The throat then is most open and the breath stream most difficult to control properly. Therefore I make it a habit to begin my practice with "oo, oh, ah, ay, ee" in succession. I never start with sustained tones. This would give my throat time to stiffen. I employ quick, soft scales, always remembering the basic principle of breath control I have mentioned, and always as though inhaling. This is an example of what I mean. To avoid shrillness on the upper tone I take the highest note with "oo" and descend with "oo."

Ex. 1

ah_____   oo_____

The same thought applied to an arpeggio would be

Ex. 2

ah_____   oo_____

These I take within comfortable limits of my voice, always remembering that the least strain is a backward step. These exercises are taken through all possible keys. There can never be too much practice of a scale or arpeggio exercise. Many singers, I know, who wonder why they do not succeed, cannot do a good scale, the very first thing they should be able to do. Every one should be like perfect pearls on a thread.

America's Fatal Ambition

One of the great troubles in America is the irrepressible ambition of both teachers and pupils. Europe is also not untinged with this. Teachers want to show results. Some teachers, I am told, start in with songs at the first or second lesson, with the sad knowledge that if they do not do this they may lose the pupil to some teacher who will peddle out songs. After four or five months I was given an operatic aria; and, of course, I sang it. A year of scales, exercises and solfeggios would have been far more time-saving. The pupils have too much to say about their education in this way. The teacher should be competent and then decide all such questions. American girls do not want this. They expect to step from vocal ignorance to a repertoire overnight. When you study voice, you should study not for two years, but realize you will never stop studying, if you wish to keep your voice. Like any others, without exercise, the singing muscles grow weak and inefficient. There are so many, many things to learn.

Of course, my whole training was that of the opera singer, and I was schooled principally in the Wagnerian roles. With the coming of the war the prejudice against the greatest anti-imperialist (with the possible exception of Beethoven) which music ever has known—the immortal Wagner— became so strong that not until now has the demand for his operas become so great that they are being resumed with wonderful success. Therefore, with the exception of a few Italian and French roles, my operatic repertoire went begging.

It was necessary for me to enter the concert field, as the management of the opera company with which I had contracts secured such engagements for me. It was like starting life anew. There is very little opportunity to show one's individuality in opera. One must play the role. Therefore I had to learn a repertoire of songs, every one of which required different treatment and different individuality. With eighteen numbers on the program, the singer has a musical, mental and vocal task which devolves entirely upon herself without the aid of chorus, co-singers, orchestra, costumes, scenery and the glamour of the footlights. It was with the greatest delight that I could fulfill the demands of the concert platform. American musical taste is very exacting. The audiences use their imagination all the time, and like romantic songs with an atmospheric background, which accounts for my great success with songs of such type as Lieurance's "By the Waters of Minnetonka." One of the greatest tasks I ever have had is that of singing my roles in many different languages. I learned some of them first in Swedish, then in Italian, then in French, then in German, then in English; as I am obliged to re-learn my Wagnerian roles now.

The road to success in voice study, like the road to success in everything else, has one compass which should be a consistent guide, and that is common sense. Avoid extremes; hold fast to your ideals; have faith in your possibilities, and work! work!! work!!!

 perspective

The Open Door to Opera

by

FLORENCE EASTON

[Biographical sketch by James Francis Cooke]

[Mme. Florence Easton was born at Middleborough, Yorkshire, England, Oct. 25th, 1887. At a very early age she was taken to Toronto, Canada, by her parents, who were both accomplished singers. She was given a musical training in youth with the view of making her a concert pianist. Her teacher was J. A. D. Tripp, and at the age of eleven she appeared in concert. Her vocal talents were discovered and she was sent to the Royal Academy at London, England, where her teachers were Reddy and Mme. Agnes Larkom, a pupil of Garcia. She then went to Paris and studied under Eliot Haslam, an English teacher resident in the French metropolis. She then took small parts in the well-known English Opera organization, the Moody-Manners Company, acquiring a large repertoire in English. With her husband, Francis Maclennen, she came to America to take the leading roles in the Savage production of *Parsifal,* remaining to sing the next season in *Madama Butterfly.* The couple were then engaged to sing for six years at the Berlin Royal Opera and became wonderfully successful. After three years at Hamburg and two years with the Chicago Opera Company she was engaged for dramatic roles at the Metropolitan, and has become a great favorite.]

What is the open door to opera in America? Is there an open door, and if not, how can one be made? Who may go through that door and what are the terms of admission? These are questions which thousands of young American opera aspirants are asking just now.

The prospect of singing at a great opera house is so alluring and the reward in money is often so great that students center their attentions upon the grand prize and are willing to take a chance of winning, even though they know that only one in a very few may succeed and then often at bitter sacrifice.

The question is a most interesting one to me, as I think that I know what the open door to opera in this country might be—what it may be if enough patriotic Americans could be found to cut through the hard walls of materialism, conventionalism and indifference. It lies through the small opera company—the only real and great school which the opera singer of the future can have.

THE SCHOOL OF *PRIME DONNE*

In European countries there are innumerable small companies capable of giving good opera which the people enjoy quite as thoroughly as the metropolitan audiences of the world enjoy the opera which commands the best singers of the times. For years these small opera companies have been the training schools of the great singers. Not to have gone through such a school was as damaging an admission as that of not having gone through a college would be to a college professor applying for a new position. Lilli Lehmann, Schumann-Heink, Ruffo, Campanini, Jenny Lind, Patti, all are graduates of these schools of practice.

In America there seems to have existed for years a kind of prejudice, bred of ignorance, against all opera companies except those employing all-star casts in the biggest theatres in the biggest cities. This existed, despite the fact that these secondary opera companies often put on opera that was superior to the best that was to be heard in some Italian, German and French cities which possessed opera companies that stood very high in the estimation of Americans who had never heard them. It was once actually the case that the fact that a singer had once sung in a smaller opera company prevented her from aspiring to sing in a great opera company. America, however, has become very much better informed and much more independent in such matters, and our opera goers are beginning to resemble European audiences in that they let their ears and their common sense determine what is best rather than their prejudices and their conventions regarding reputation. It was actually the case at one time in America that a singer with a great reputation could command a large audience, whereas a singer of far greater ability and infinitely better voice might be shut out because she had once sung in an opera company not as pretentious as those in the big cities. This seemed very comic indeed to many European singers, who laughed in their coat sleeves over the real situation.

In the first place, the small companies in many cities would provide more singers with opportunities for training and public appearances. The United States now has two or three major opera companies. Count upon your fingers the greatest number of singers who could be accommodated with parts: only once or twice in a decade does the young singer, at the age when the best formative work must be done, have a chance to attain the leading roles. If we had in America ten or twenty smaller opera companies of real merit, the chances would be greatly multiplied.

The first thing that the singer has to fight is stage fright. No matter how well you may know a role in a studio, unless you are a very extraordinary person you are likely to take months in acquiring the stage freedom and ease in working before an audience. There is only one cure for stage fright, and that is to appear continually until it wears off. Many deserving singers have lost their great chances because they have depended upon what they have learned in the studio only to find that when they went before a great and critical audience their ability was suddenly reduced to 10 per cent if not to zero. Even after years of practice and experience in great European opera houses where I appeared repeatedly before royalty, the reputation of the Metropolitan Opera House in New York was so great that at the time I made my debut there I was so afflicted by stage fright that my voice was actually reduced to one-half of its force and my other abilities accordingly. This is the truth, and I am glad to have young singers know it as it emphasizes my point.

Imagine what the effect would have been upon a young singer who had never before sung in public on the stage. Footlight paralysis is one of the most terrifying of all acute diseases and there is no cure for it but experience.

THE BEST BEGINNING

In the Moody-Manners Company in England, the directors wisely understood this situation and prepared for it. All the singers scheduled to take leading roles (and they were for the most part very young singers, since when the singer became experienced enough she was immediately stolen by companies paying higher salaries) were expected to go for a certain time in the chorus (not to sing, just to walk off and on the stage) until familiar with the situation. Accordingly, my first appearance with the Moody-Manners Company was when I walked out with the chorus. I have never heard of this being done deliberately by any other managers, but think how sensible it is!

Again, it is far more advantageous for the young singer to appear in the smaller opera house at first, so that if any errors are made the opera goers will not be unforgiving. There is no tragedy greater than throwing a young girl into an operatic situation far greater than her experience and ability can meet, and then condemning her for years because she did not rise to the occasion. This has happened many times in recent years. Ambition is a beautiful thing; but when ambition induces one to walk upon a tight rope over Niagara, without having first learned to walk properly on earth, ambition should be restrained. I can recollect several singers who were widely heralded at their first performances by enthusiastic admirers, who are now no longer known. What has become of them? Is it not better to learn the profession of opera singing in its one great school, and learn it so thoroughly that one can advance in the profession, just as one may advance in every other profession? The singer in the small opera company who, night after night, says to herself, "To-morrow it must be better," is the one who will be the Lilli Lehmann, the Galli-Curci, or the Schumann-Heink of to-morrow; not the important person who insists upon postponing her debut until she can appear at the Metropolitan or at Covent Garden.

Colonel Henry W. Savage did America an immense service, as did the Aborn Brothers and Fortune Gallo, in helping to create a popular taste for opera presented in a less pretentious form. America needs such companies and needs them badly, not merely to educate the public up to an appreciation of the fact that the finest operatic performances in the world are now being given at the Metropolitan Opera House, but to help provide us with well-schooled singers for the future.

NECESSITY OF ROUTINE

Nothing can take the place of routine in learning operas. Many, many opera singers I have known seem to be woefully lacking in it. In learning a new opera, I learn all the parts that have anything to do with the part I am expected to sing. In other words, I find it very inadvisable to depend upon cues. There are so many disturbing things constantly occurring on the stage to throw one off one's track. For instance, when I made my first appearance in Mascagni's *Lodoletta* I was obliged to go on with only twenty-four hours' notice, without rehearsal, in an opera I had seen produced only once. I had studied the role only two weeks. While on the stage I was so entranced with the wonderful singing of Mr. Caruso that I forgot to come in at the right time. He said to me quickly *sotto voce*—

"Canta! Canta! Canta!"

And my routine drill of the part enabled me to come in without letting the audience know of my error.

The mere matter of getting the voice to go with the orchestra, as well as that of identifying cues heard in the unusual quality of the orchestral instruments (so different from the tone quality of the piano), is most confusing, and only routine can accustom one to being ready to meet all of these strange conditions.

One is supposed to keep an eye on the conductor practically all of the time while singing. The best singers are those who never forget this, but do it so artfully that the audience never suspects. Many singers follow the conductor's baton so conspicuously that they give the appearance of monkeys on a string. This, of course, is highly ludicrous. I don't know of any way of overcoming it but experience. Yes, there is another great help, and that is musicianship. The conductor who knows that an artist is a musician in fact is immensely relieved and always very appreciative. Singers should learn as much about the technical side of music as possible. Learning to play the violin or the piano, and learning to play it well is invaluable.

WATCHING FOR OPPORTUNITIES

The singer must be ever on the alert for opportunities to advance. This is largely a matter of preparation. If one is capable, the opportunities usually come. I wonder if I may relate a little incident which occurred to me in Germany long before the war. I had been singing in Berlin, when the impresario of the Royal Opera approached me and asked me if I could sing *Aïda* on a following Monday. I realized that if I admitted that I had never sung *Aïda* before, the thoroughgoing, matter-of-fact German Intendant would never even let me have a chance. Emmy Destinn was then the prima donna at the Royal Opera, and had been taken ill. The post was one of the operatic plums of all Europe. Before I knew it I had said, "Yes, I can sing *Aïda*." It was a white lie, and once told, I had to live up to it. I had never sung *Aïda,* and only knew part of it. Running home I worked all night long to learn the last act. Over and over the role hundreds and hundreds of times I went, until it seemed as though my eyes would drop out of my head. Monday night came, and thanks to my routine experience in smaller companies, I had learned *Aïda* so that I was perfectly confident of it. Imagine the strain, however, when I learned that the Kaiser and the court were to be present. At the end I was called before the Kaiser, who, after warmly complimenting me, gave me the greatly coveted post in his opera house. I do not believe that he ever found out that the little Toronto girl had actually fibbed her way into an opportunity.

TALES OF STRAUSS

Strauss was one of the leading conductors while I was at the Royal Opera and I sang under his baton many, many times. He was a real genius—in that once his art work was completed, his interest immediately centered

upon the next. Once while we were performing *Rosenkavalier* he came behind the scenes and said:

"Will this awfully *long* opera never end? I want to go home." I said to
him, "But Doctor, you composed it yourself," and he said, "Yes, but I
never meant to conduct it."

Let it be explained that Strauss was an inveterate player of the German
card game Scat, and would far rather seek a quiet corner with a few choice
companions than go through one of his own works night after night.
However, whenever the creative instinct was at work he let nothing im-
pede it. I remember seeing him write upon his cuffs (no doubt some passing theme) during a performance of *Meistersinger* he was conducting.

The Singer's Greatest Need

The singer's greatest need, or his greatest asset if he has one, is an honest critic. My husband and I have made it a point never to miss hearing
one another sing, no matter how many times we have heard each other
sing in a role. Sometimes, after a big performance, it is very hard to have
to be told about all the things that one did not do well, but that is the only
way to improve. There are always many people to tell one the good things,
but I feel that the biggest help that I have had through my career has been
the help of my husband, because he has always told me the places where I
could improve, so that every performance I had something new to think
about. An artist never stands still. He either goes forward or backward and,
of course, the only way to get to the top is by going forward.

The difficulty in America is in giving the young singers a chance after
their voices are placed. If only we could have a number of excellent stock
opera companies, even though there had to be a few traveling stars after
the manner of the old dramatic companies, where everybody had to start
at the bottom and work his way up, because with a lovely voice, talent and
perseverance any one can get to the top if one has a chance to work. By
"work" I mean singing as many new roles as possible and as often as possible and not starting at a big opera house singing perhaps two or three
times during a season. Just think of it—the singer at a small opera house
has more chance to learn in two months than the beginner at a big opera
house might have in five years. After all, the thing that is most valuable to
a singer is time, as with time the voice will diminish in beauty. Getting to
the top via the big opera house is the work of a lifetime, and the golden
tones are gone before one really has an opportunity to do one's best work.

The Will to Succeed—a Compelling Force

An interview with
GERALDINE FARRAR

by Harriette Brower

"To measure the importance of Geraldine Farrar (at the Metropolitan Opera House, New York) one has only to think of the void there would have been during the last decade, and more, if she had not been there. Try to picture the period between 1906 and 1920 without Farrar—it is inconceivable! Farrar, more than any other singer, has been the triumphant living symbol of the new day for the American artist at the Metropolitan. She paved the way. Since that night, in 1906, when her Juliette stirred the staid old house, American singers have been added year by year to the personnel. Among these younger singers there are those who will admit at once that it was the success of Geraldine Farrar which gave them the impetus to work hard for a like success."

These thoughts have been voiced by a recent reviewer, and will find a quick response from young singers all over the country, who have been inspired by the career of this representative artist, and by the thousands who have enjoyed her singing and her many characterizations.

I was present on the occasion of Miss Farrar's debut at the greatest opera house of her home land. I, too, was thrilled by the fresh young voice in the girlish and charming impersonation of Juliette. It is a matter of history that from the moment of her auspicious return to America she has been constantly before the public, from the beginning to end of each operatic season. Other singers often come for part of the season, step out and make room for others. But Miss Farrar, as well as Mr. Caruso, can be depended on to remain.

Any one who gives the question a moment's thought, knows that such a career, carried through a score of years, means constant, unremitting labor. There must be daily work on vocal technic; repertoire must be kept up to opera pitch, and last and perhaps most important of all, new works must be sought, studied and assimilated.

The singer who can accomplish these tasks will have little or no time for society and the gay world, inasmuch as her strength must be devoted to the service of her art. She must keep healthy hours, be always ready to appear, and never disappoint her audiences. And such, according to Miss Farrar's own words, is her record in the service of art.

While zealously guarding her time from interruption from the merely curious, Miss Farrar does not entrench herself behind insurmountable barriers, as many singers seem to do, so that no honest seeker for her views of study and achievement can find her. While making a rule not to try voices of the throng of young singers who would like to have her verdict on their ability and prospects, Miss Farrar is very gracious to those who really need to see her. Again—unlike others—she will make an appointment a couple of weeks in advance, and one can rest assured she will keep that appointment to the day and hour, in spite of many pressing calls on her attention.

To meet and talk for an hour with an artist who has so often charmed you from the other side of the footlights, is a most interesting experience. In the present instance it began with my being taken up to Miss Farrar's private sanctum, at the top of her New York residence. Though this is her den, where she studies and works, it is a spacious parlor, where all is light, color, warmth and above all, *quiet*. A thick crimson carpet hushes the footfall. A luxurious couch piled with silken cushions, and comfortable arm chairs are all in the same warm tint; over the grand piano is thrown a cover of red velvet, gold embroidered. Portraits of artists and many costly trifles are scattered here and there. The young lady who acts as secretary happened to be in the room and spoke with enthusiasm of the singer's absorption in her work, her delight in it, her never-failing energy and good spirits. "From the day I heard Miss Farrar sing I felt drawn to her and hoped the time would come when I could serve her in some way. I did not know then that it would be in this way. Her example is an inspiration to all who come in touch with her."

In a few moments Miss Farrar herself appeared, and the young girl withdrew.

And was this Farrar who stood before me, in the flush of vigorous womanhood, and who welcomed me so graciously? The first impression was one of friendliness and sincerity, which caused the artist for the moment to be forgotten in the unaffected simplicity of the woman.

Miss Farrar settled herself comfortably among the red silk cushions and was ready for our talk. The simplicity of manner was reflected in her words. She did not imply—there is only one right way, and I have found it. "These things seem best for my voice, and this is the way I work. But, since each voice is different, they might not fit any one else. I have no desire to lay down rules for others; I can only speak of my own experience.

THE QUESTION OF HEALTH

"And you would first know how I keep strong and well and always ready? Perhaps the answer is, I keep regular hours and habits, and love my work. I have always loved to sing, as far back as I can remember. Music means everything to me—it is my life. As a child and young girl, I was the despair of my playmates because I would not join their games; I did not care to skate, play croquet or tennis, or such things. I never wanted to exercise violently, and, to me, unnecessarily, because it interfered with my singing; took energy which I thought might be better applied. As I grew older I did not care to keep late hours and be in an atmosphere where people smoked and perhaps drank, for these things were bad for my voice and I could not do my work next day. My time is always regularly laid out. I rise at half past seven, and am ready to work at nine. I do not care to sit up late at night, either, for I think late hours react on the voice. Occasionally, if we have a few guests for dinner, I ask them, when ten thirty arrives, to stay as long as they wish and enjoy themselves, but I retire.

TECHNICAL STUDY

"There are gifted people who may be called natural-born singers. Melba is one of these. Such singers do not require much technical practice, or if they need a little of it, half an hour a day is sufficient. I am not one of those who do not need to practice. I give between one and two hours daily to vocalises, scales and tone study. But I love it! A scale is beautiful to me, if it is rightly sung. In fact it is not merely a succession of notes; it represents color. I always translate sound into color. It is a fascinating study to make different qualities of tonal color in the voice. Certain roles require an entirely different range of colors from others. One night I must sing a part with thick, heavy, rich tones; the next night my tones must be thinned out in quite another timbre of the voice, to fit an opposite character."

Asked if she can hear herself, Miss Farrar answered:

"No, I do not actually hear my voice, except in a general way; but we learn to know the sensations produced in muscles of throat, head, face, lips and other parts of the anatomy, which vibrate in a certain manner to correct tone production. We learn the *feeling* of the tone. Therefore every one, no matter how advanced, requires expert advice as to the results.

WITH LEHMANN

"I have studied for a long time with Lilli Lehmann in Berlin; in fact I might say she is almost my only teacher, though I did have some instruction before going to her, both in America and Paris. You see, I always sang, even as a very little girl'. My mother has excellent taste and knowledge in music, and finding I was in danger of straining my voice through singing with those older than myself, she placed me with a vocal teacher when I was twelve, as a means of preservation.

"Lehmann is a wonderful teacher and an extraordinary woman as well. What art is there—what knowledge and understanding! What intensity there is in everything she does. She used to say: 'Remember, these four walls which inclose you, make a very different space to fill compared to an opera house; you must take this fact into consideration and study accordingly'. No one ever said a truer word. If one only studies or sings in a room or studio, one has no idea of what it means to fill a theater. It is a distinct branch of one's work to gain power and control and to adapt one's self to large spaces. One can only learn this by doing it.

"It is sometimes remarked by listeners at the opera, that we sing too loud, or that we scream. They surely never think of the great size of the stage, of the distance from the proscenium arch to the footlights, or from the arch to the first set of wings. They do not consider that within recent years the size of the orchestra has been largely increased, so that we are obliged to sing against this great number of instruments, which are making every possible kind of a noise except that of a siren. It is no wonder that we must make much effort to be heard: sometimes the effort may seem injudicious. The point we must consider is to make the greatest possible effect with the least possible exertion.

"Lehmann is the most painstaking, devoted teacher a young singer can have. It is proof of her excellent method and her perfect understanding of vocal mastery, that she is still able to sing in public, if not with her old-time power, yet with good tone quality. It shows what an artist she really is. I always went over to her every summer, until the war came. We would work together at her villa in Gruenewald, which you yourself know. Or we would go for a holiday down nearer Salzburg, and would work there. We always worked wherever we were.

MEMORIZING

"How do I memorize? I play the song or role through a number of times, concentrating on both words and music at once. I am a pianist anyway; and committing to memory is very easy for me. I was trained to learn by heart from the very start. When I sang my little songs at six years old, mother would never let me have any music before me: I must know my songs by heart. And so I learned them quite naturally. To me singing was like talking to people.

CONTRASTING COLORATURA AND DRAMATIC SINGING

"You ask me to explain the difference between the coloratura and the dramatic organ. I should say it is a difference of timbre. The coloratura voice is bright and brilliant in its higher portion, but becomes weaker and thinner as it descends; whereas the dramatic voice has a thicker, richer quality all through, especially in its lower register. The coloratura voice will sing upper C, and it will sound very high indeed. I might sing the same tone, but it would sound like A flat, because the tone would be of such totally different timbre.

TO THE YOUNG SINGER

"If I have any message to the young singer, it would be: Stick to your work and study systematically, whole-heartedly. If you do not love your work enough to give it your best thought, to make sacrifices for it, there is something wrong with you. Then choose some other line of work, to which you can give undivided attention and devotion. For music requires this. As for sacrifices, they really do not exist, if they promote the thing you honestly love most.

"Do not fancy you can properly prepare yourself in a short time to undertake a musical career, for the path is a long and arduous one. You must never stop studying, for there is always so much to learn. If I have sung a role a hundred times, I always find places that can be improved; indeed I never sing a role twice exactly in the same way. So, from whatever side you consider the singer's work and career, both are of absorbing interest.

"Another thing; do not worry, for that is bad for your voice. If you have not made this tone correctly, or sung that phrase to suit yourself, pass it over for the moment with a wave of the hand or a smile; but don't become discouraged. Go right on! I knew a beautiful American in Paris who possessed a lovely voice. But she had a very sensitive nature, which could not endure hard knocks. She began to worry over little failures and disappointments, with the result that in three years her voice was quite gone. We must not give way to disappointments, but conquer them, and keep right along the path we have started on.

MODERN MUSIC

"Modern music requires quite a different handling of the voice and makes entirely different demands upon it than does the older music. The old Italian operas required little or no action, only beautiful singing. The opera houses were smaller and so were the orchestras. The singer could stand still in the middle of the stage and pour out beautiful tones, with few movements of body to mar his serenity. But we, in these days, demand action as well as song. We need singing actors and actresses. The music is declamatory; the singer must throw his whole soul into his part, must act as well as sing. Things are all on a larger scale. It is a far greater strain on the voice to interpret one of the modern Italian operas than to sing one of those quietly beautiful works of the old school.

"America's growth in music has been marvelous on the appreciative and interpretive side. With such a musical awakening, we can look forward to the appearance of great creative genius right here in this country, perhaps in the near future. Why should we not expect it? We have not yet produced a composer who can write enduring operas or symphonies. MacDowell is our highest type as yet; but others will come who will carry the standard higher.

Voice Limitations

"The singer must be willing to admit limitations of voice and style and not attempt parts which do not come within the compass of her attainments. Neither is it wise to force the voice up or down when it seems a great effort to do so. We can all think of singers whose natural quality is mezzo—let us say—who try to force the voice up into a higher register. There is one artist of great dramatic gifts, who not content with the rich quality of her natural organ, tried to add several high notes to the upper portion. The result was disastrous. Again, some of our young singers who possess beautiful, sweet voices, should not force them to the utmost limit of power, simply to fill, or try to fill a great space. The life of the voice will be impaired by such injurious practice.

Vocal Mastery

"What do I understand by 'vocal mastery'? It is something very difficult to define. For a thing that is mastered must be really perfect. To master vocal art, the singer must have so developed his voice that it is under complete control; then he can do with it whatsoever he wishes. He must be able to produce all he desires of power, pianissimo, accent, shading, delicacy and variety of color. Who is equal to the task?"

Miss Farrar was silent a moment; then she said, answering her own question:

"I can think of but two people who honestly can be said to possess vocal mastery: they are Caruso and McCormack. Those who have only heard the latter do little Irish tunes, have no idea of what he is capable. I have heard him sing Mozart as no one else I know of can. These two artists have, through ceaseless application, won vocal mastery. It is something we are all striving for!"

Teaching Yourself to Sing

by

AMELITA GALLI-CURCI

[Biographical sketch by James Francis Cooke]

[Mme. Galli-Curci was born at Milan, November 18th, 1889, of a family distinguished in the arts and in the professions. She entered the Milan Conservatory, winning the first prize and diploma in piano playing in 1903. For a time after her graduation she toured as a pianist and then resolved to become a singer. She is practically self-taught in the vocal art. Her debut was made in Rome at the Teatro Constanzi, in the role of Gilda in *Rigoletto*. She was pronouncedly successful from the very start. During the next six years she sang principally in Italy, South America (three tours), and in Spain, her success increasing with every appearance. In 1916 she appeared at Chicago with the Chicago Opera Company, creating a furor. The exceptionally beautiful records of her interpretations created an immense demand to hear her in concert, and her successes everywhere have been historic. Not since Patti has there been a singer upon whom such wide-spread critical comment has been made in praise of her exquisite velvety quality of tone, vocal technic and interpretative intelligence. Hailed as "Patti's only successor," she has met with greater popular success in opera and concert than any of the singers of recent years. In 1921 she married the gifted American composer Homer Samuels, who for many years had been the pianist upon her tours.]

Just what influence heredity may have upon the musical art and upon musicians has, of course, been a much discussed question. In my own case, I was fortunate in having a father who, although engaged in another vocation, was a fine amateur musician. My grandfather was a conductor and my grandmother was an opera singer of distinction in Italy. Like myself, she was a coloratura soprano, and I can recollect with joy her voice and her method of singing. Even at the age of seventy-five her voice was wonderfully well preserved, because she always sang with the greatest ease and with none of the forced throat restrictions which make the work of so many singers insufferable.

My own musical education began at the age of five, when I commenced to play the piano. Meanwhile I sang around the house, and my grandmother used to say in good humor: "Keep it up, my dear; perhaps some day you may be a better singer than I am." My father, however, was more seriously interested in instrumental music, and desired that I should become a pianist.

How fortunate for me! Otherwise, I should never have had that thorough musical drill which gave me an acquaintance with the art which I cannot believe could come in any other way. Mascagni was a very good friend of our family and took a great interest in my playing. He came to our house very frequently, and his advice and inspiration naturally meant much to a young, impressionable girl.

GENERAL EDUCATION

My general education was very carefully guarded by my father, who sent me to the best schools in Milan, one of which was under the management of Germans, and it was there that I acquired my acquaintance with the German language. I was then sent to the Conservatorio, and graduated with a gold medal as a pianist. This won me some distinction in Italy and enabled me to tour as a pianist. I did not pretend to play the big, exhaustive works, but my programs were made up of such pieces as the *ABEGG Variations* of Schumann, studies by Scharwenka, impromptus of Chopin, the four scherzos of Chopin, the first ballade, the nocturnes (the fifth in the book was my favorite) and works of Bach. (Of course, I had been through the *Wohltemperierte Klavier.*) In those days I was very frail, and I had aspired to develop my repertoire so that later I could include the great works for the piano requiring a more or less exhaustive technic of the bravura type.

Once I went to hear Busoni, and after the concert, came to me like a revelation, "You can never be such a pianist as he. Your hand and your physical strength will not permit it." I went home in more or less sadness, knowing that despite the success I had had in my piano playing, my decision was a wise one. Figuratively, I closed the lid of my piano upon my career as a pianist and decided to learn how to sing. The memory of my grandmother's voice singing Bellini's "Qui la voce" was still ringing in my ears with the lovely purity of tone that she possessed. Mascagni called upon us at that time, and I asked him to hear me sing. He did so, and threw up his hands, saying, "Why in the world have you been wasting your time with piano playing when you have a natural voice like that? Such voices are born. Start to work at once to develop your voice." Meanwhile, of course, I had heard a great deal of singing and a great deal of so-called voice teaching. I went to two teachers in Milan, but was so dissatisfied with what I heard from them and from their pupils that I was determined that it would be necessary for me to develop my own voice. Please do not take this as an inference that all vocal teachers are bad or are dispensable. My own case was peculiar. I had been saturated with musical traditions since my babyhood. I had had, in addition, a very fine musical training. Of course, without this I could not have attempted to do what I did in the way of self-training. Nevertheless, it is my firm conviction that unless the student of singing has in his brain and in his soul those powers of judging for himself whether the quality of a tone, the intonation (pitch), the shading, the purity and the resonance are what they should be to insure the highest artistic results, it will be next to impossible for him to secure these. This is what is meant by the phrase—"Singers are born and not made." The power of discrimination, the judgment, etc., must be inherent. No teacher can possibly give them to a pupil, except in an artificial way. That, possibly, is the reason why so many students sing like parrots: because they have the power of mimicry, but nothing comes from within. The fine teacher can, of course, take a fine sense of tonal values, etc., and, provided the student has a really good natural voice, lead him to reveal to himself the ways in which he can use his voice to the best advantage. Add to this a fine musical training, and we have a singer. But no teacher can give to a voice that velvety smoothness, that liquid fluency, that bell-like clarity which the ear of the educated musician expects, and which the public at large demands, unless the student has the power of determining for himself what is good and what is bad.

FOUR YEARS OF HARD TRAINING

It was no easy matter to give up the gratifying success which attended my pianistic appearances to begin a long term of self-study, self-development. Yet I realized that it would hardly be possible for me to accomplish what I desired in less than four years. Therefore, I worked daily for four years, drilling myself with the greatest care in scales, arpeggios and sustained tones. The coloratura facility I seemed to possess naturally, to a certain extent; but I realized that only by hard and patient work would it be possible to have all my runs, trills, etc., so that they always would be smooth, articulate and free—that is, unrestricted—at any time. I studied the roles in which I aspired to appear, and attended the opera faithfully to hear fine singing, as well as bad singing.

As the work went on it became more and more enjoyable. I felt that I was upon the right path, and that meant everything. If I had continued as a pianist I could never have been more than a mediocrity, and that I could not have tolerated.

About this time came a crisis in my father's business; it became necessary for me to teach. Accordingly, I took a number of piano pupils and enjoyed that phase of my work very much indeed. I gave lessons for four years, and in my spare time worked with my voice, all by myself, with my friend, the piano. My guiding principles were:

There must be as little consciousness of effort in the throat as possible.
There must always be the Joy of Singing.

Success is based upon sensation, whether it feels right to me in my mouth, in my throat, that I know, and nobody else can tell me.

I remember that my grandmother, who sang "Una voce poco fa" at seventy-five, always cautioned me to never force a single tone. I did not study exercises like those of Concone, Panofka, Bordogni, etc., because they seemed to me a waste of time in my case. I did not require musical knowledge, but needed special drill. I knew where my weak spots were. What was the use of vocal studies which required me to do a lot of work and only occasionally touched those portions of my voice which needed special attention? Learning a repertoire was a great task in itself, and there was no time to waste upon anything I did not actually need. Because of the natural fluency I have mentioned, I devoted most of my time to slower exercises at first. What could be simpler than this?

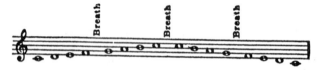

These, of course, were sung in the most convenient range in my voice. The more rapid exercises I took from C to F above the treble staff.

Even to this day I sing up to high F every day, in order that I may be sure that I have the tones to E below in public work. Another exercise which I used very frequently was this, in the form of a trill. Great care was taken to have the intonation (pitch) absolutely accurate in the rapid passages, as well as in the slow passages.

When I had reached a certain point, I determined that it might be possible for me to get an engagement. I was then twenty, and my dear mother was horrified at the idea of my going on the stage so young. She was afraid of evil influences. In my own mind I realized that evil was everywhere, in business, society, everywhere, and that if one was to keep out of dirt and come out clean, one must make one's art the object first of all. Art is so great, so all-consuming, that any one with a deep reverence for its beauties, its grandeur, can have but little time for the lower things of life. All that an artist calls for in his soul is to be permitted to work at his best in his art. Then, and then only, is he happiest. Because of my mother's opposition, and because I felt I was strong enough to resist the temptations which she knew I might encounter, I virtually eloped with a copy of *Rigoletto* under my arm and made my way for the Teatro Constanzi, the leading opera house of Rome.

I might readily have secured letters from influential musical friends, such as Mascagni and others, but I determined that it would be best to secure an engagement upon my own merits, if I could, and then I would know whether or not I was really prepared to make my debut, or whether I had better study more. I went to the manager's office and, appealing to his business sense, told him that, as I was a young unknown singer, he could secure my services for little money, and begged for permission to sing for him. I knew he was beset by such requests, but he immediately gave me a hearing, and I was engaged for one performance of *Rigoletto*. The night of the debut came, and I was obliged to sing "Caro nome" again in response to a vociferous encore. This was followed by other successes, and I was engaged for two years for a South American tour, under the direction of my good friend and adviser, the great operatic director Mugnone. In South America there was enthusiasm everywhere, but all the time I kept working constantly with my voice, striving to perfect details.

At the end of the South American tour I desired to visit New York and find out what America was like. Because of the war Europe was operatically impossible (it was 1916), but I had not the slightest idea of singing in the United States just then. By merest accident I ran into an American friend (Mr. Thorner) on Broadway. He had heard me sing in Italy, and immediately took me to Maestro Campanini, who was looking then for a coloratura soprano to sing for only two performances in Chicago, as the remainder of his program was filled for the year. This was in the springtime, and it meant that I was to remain in New York until October and November. The opportunity seemed like an unusual accident of fate, and I resolved to stay, studying my own voice all the while to improve it more and more. October and the debut in *Rigoletto* came. The applause astounded me; it was electric, like a thunderstorm. No one was more astonished than I. Engagements and offers came from everywhere, but not enough, I hope, to ever induce me not to believe that in the vocal art one must continually strive for higher and higher goals. Laziness, indifference and lassitude which come with success are the ruin of Art and the artist. The normal healthy artist with the right ideals never reaches his zenith. If he did, or if he thought he did, his career would come to a sudden end.

☙

The Know How in the Art of Singing

by

MARY GARDEN

[Biographical sketch by James Francis Cooke]

[Mary Garden was born February 20th, 1877, in Aberdeen, Scotland. She came to America with her parents when she was eight years of age and was brought up in Chicopee, Massachusetts, Hartford, Connecticut, and Chicago, Illinois. She studied the violin when she was six and the piano when she was twelve. It was the ambition of her parents to make her an instrumental performer. She studied voice with Mrs. S. R. Duff, who in time took her to Paris and placed her under the instruction of Trabadello and Lucien Fugère. Her operatic debut was made in Charpentier's *Louise* at the Opéra Comique in 1900. Her success was immediate both as an actress and as a singer. She was chosen by Debussy and others for especially intricate roles. She created the role of Mélisande; also, Fiammette in Leroux's *La Reine Fiammette*. In 1907 she made her American debut in *Thaïs* at the Manhattan Opera House in New York City. Later she accepted leading roles with the Philadelphia-Chicago Opera Co. She is considered by many the finest singing actress living—her histrionic gifts being in every way equal to her vocal gifts. In 1921 she was made the manager of the Chicago Opera Company.]

The modern opera singer cannot content herself merely with the "know how" of singing. That is, she must be able to know so much more than the mere elemental facts of voice production that it would take volumes to give an intimation of the real requirements.

The girl who wants to sing in opera must have one thought and one thought only—"What will contribute to my musical, histrionic and artistic success?"

Unless the "career" comes first there is not likely to be any "career."
I wonder if the public ever realizes what this sacrifice means to an artiste—to a woman.

Of course, there are great recompenses—the thrill that comes with artistic triumphs—the sensations that accompany achievement—who but the artist can know what this means—the joy of bringing to life some great masterpiece?

Music manifests itself in children at a very early age. It is very rare indeed that it comes to the surface later in life. I was always musical. Only the media changed—one time it was violin, then piano, then voice. The dolls of my sisters only annoyed me because I could not tolerate dolls. They seemed a waste of time to me, and when they had paper dolls, I would go into the room when nobody was looking and cut the dolls' heads off. I have never been able to account for my delight in doing this.

My father was musical. He wanted me to be a musician, but he had little thought at first of my being a singer. Accordingly, at eight I was possessed of a fiddle. This meant more to me than all the dolls in the world. Oh, how I loved that violin, which I could make speak just by drawing a bow over it! There was something worth while.

I was only as big as a minute, and, of course, as soon as I could play the routine things of de Bériot, variations and the like, I was considered one of those abominable things, "an infant prodigy."

I was brought out to play for friends and any musical person who could stand it. Then I gave a concert, and my father saw the finger of destiny pointing to my career as a great violinist.

To me the finger of destiny pointed the other way; because I immediately sickened of the violin and dropped it forever. Yes, I could play now if I had to, but you probably wouldn't want to hear me.

Ah, but I do play. I play every time I sing. The violin taught me the need for perfect intonation, fluency in execution, ever so many things.

Then came the piano. Here was a new artistic toy. I worked very hard with it. My sister and I went back to Aberdeen for a season of private school, and I kept up my piano until I could play acceptably many of the best-known compositions, Grieg, Chopin, etc., being my favorites. I was never a very fine pianist, understand me, but the piano unlocked the doors to thousands of musical treasure houses—admitted me to musical literature through the main gate, and has been of invaluable aid to me in my career. See my fingers, how long and thin they are—of course, I was a capable pianist—long, supple fingers, combined with my musical experience gained in violin playing, made that certain.

Then I dropped the piano. Dropped it at once. Its possibilities stood revealed before me, and they were not to be the limit of my ambitions.

For the girl who hopes to be an operatic "star" there could be nothing better than a good drilling in violin or piano. The girl has no business to sing while she is yet a child—and she is that until she is sixteen or over. Better let her work hard getting a good general education and a good musical education. The voice will keep, and it will be sweeter and fresher if it is not overused in childhood.

Once, with my heart set upon becoming a singer, my father fortunately took me to Mrs. Robinson Duff, of Chicago. To her, my mentor to this day, I owe much of my vocal success. I was very young and very emotional, with a long pigtail down my back. At first the work did not enrapture me, for I could not see the use of spending so much time upon breathing. Now I realize what it did for me.

What should the girl starting singing avoid? First, let her avoid an incompetent teacher. There are teachers, for instance, who deliberately teach the "stroke of the glottis" (*coup de glotte*).

What is the stroke of the glottis? The lips of the vocal cords in the larynx are pressed together so that the air becomes compressed behind them and instead of coming out in a steady, unimpeded stream, it causes a kind of explosion. Say the word "up" in the throat very forcibly and you will get the right idea.

This is a most pernicious habit. Somehow, it crept into some phases of vocal teaching, and has remained. It leads to a constant irritation of the throat and ruin to the vocal organs.

When I went to Paris, Mrs. Duff took me to many of the leading vocal teachers of the city, and said, "Now, Mary, I want you to use your own judgment in picking out a teacher, because if you don't like the teacher you will not succeed."

Thus we went around from studio to studio. One asked me to do this—to hum—to make funny, unnatural noises, anything but sing. Finally, Trabadello, now retired to his country home, really asked me to sing in a normal, natural way, not as a freak. I said to myself, "This is the teacher for me." I could not have had a better one.

Look out for teachers with freak methods—ten to one they are making you one of their experiments. There is nothing that any voice teacher has ever found superior to giving simple scales and exercises sung upon the syllables "lah" ("ah" as in *harbor*), "leh" ("eh" as in *they*), "lee" ("ee" as in *me*). With a good teacher to keep watch over the breathing and the quality, "what more can one have?"

I have always believed in a great many scales and in a great deal of singing florid roles in Italian. Italian is inimitable for the singer. The dulcet, velvet-like character of the language gives something which nothing else can impart. It does not make any difference whether you purpose singing in French, German, English, Russian or Sudanese, you will gain much from exercising in Italian.

Staccato practice is valuable. Here is an exercise which I take nearly every day of my life:

The staccato must be controlled from the diaphragm, however, and this comes only after a great deal of work.

Three-quarters of an hour a day practice suffices me. I find it injurious to practice too long. But I study for hours. Such a role as Aphrodite* I take quietly and sing it over mentally time and time again without making a sound. I study the harmonies, the nuances, the phrasing, the breathing, so that when the time for singing it comes I know it and do not waste my voice by going over it time and again, as some singers do. In the end I find that I know it better for this kind of study.

The study of acting has been a very personal matter with me. I have never been through any courses of study, such as that given in dramatic schools. This may do for some people, but it would have been impossible for me. There must be technic in all forms of art, but it has always seemed to me that acting was one of the arts in which the individual must make his own technic. I have seen many representatives of the schools of acting here and abroad. Sometimes their performances, based upon technical studies of the art, result in superb acting. Again, their work is altogether indifferent. Technic in acting is more likely to suppress than to inspire. If acting is not inspired, it is nothing. I study the human emotions that would naturally underlie the scene in which I am placed—then I think what one would be most likely to do under such conditions. When the actual time of appearance on the stage arrives, I forget all about this and make myself the person of the role.

[*Camille Erlanger's opera *Aphrodite* was first performed in America, in February 1921, by the Chicago Opera Association with Mary Garden in the title role.]

This is the Italian method rather than the French. There are, to my mind, no greater actors living than Duse and Zacchona, and they are both exponents of the natural method that I employ.

Great acting has always impressed me wonderfully. I went from Paris to London repeatedly to see Beerbohm Tree in his best roles. Sir Herbert was not always uniformly fine, but he was a great actor and I learned much from watching him. Once I induced Debussy to make the trip to see him act. Debussy was delighted.

Debussy! Ah, what a rare genius—my greatest friend in Art! Everything he wrote we went over together. He was a terribly exacting master. Few people in America realize what a transcendent pianist he was. The piano seemed to be thinking, feeling, vibrating while he was at the keyboard. Time and again we went over his principal works, note for note. Now and then he would stop and clasp his hands over his face in sudden silence, repeating, "It is all wrong—it is all wrong." But he was too good a teacher to let it go at that. He could tell me exactly what was wrong and how to remedy it. When I first sang for him, at the time when they were about to produce *Pelleas and Mélisande* at the Opéra Comique, I thought that I had not pleased him. But I learned later that he had said to M. Carré, the director: "Don't look for anyone else." From that time he and his family became my close friends. The fatalistic side of our meeting seemed to interest him very much. "To think," he used to say, "that you were born in Aberdeen, Scotland, lived in America all those years and should come to Paris to create my Mélisande!"

As I have said, Debussy was a gorgeous pianist. He could play with the greatest delicacy and could play in the leonine fashion of Rubinstein. He was familiar with Beethoven, Bach, Handel and the classics, and was devoted to them. Wagner he could not abide. He called him a "griffe papier"—a scribbler. He thought that he had no importance in the world of music, and to mention Wagner to him was like waving a red flag before a bull.

It is difficult to account for such an opinion. Wagner, to me, is the great tone colorist, the master of orchestral wealth and dramatic intensity. Sometimes I have been so Wagner-hungry that I have not known what to do. For years I went every year to Munich to see the wonderful performances at the Prinzregenten Theater.

In closing let me say that it seems to me a great deal of the failure among young singers is that they are too impatient to acquire the "know how." They want to blossom out on the first night as great prima donnas, without any previous experience. How ridiculous this is! I worked for a whole year at the Opera Comique, at $100 a month, singing such a trying opera as *Louise* two and three times a week. When they raised me to $175 a month I thought that I was rich, and when $400 a month came, my fortune had surely been made! All this time I was gaining precious experience. It could not have come to me in any other way. As I have said, the natural school—the natural school, like that of the Italians—stuffed as it is with glorious red blood instead of the white bones of technic in the misunderstood sense, was the only possible school for me. If our girls would only stop hoping to make a debut at $1,000 a night and get down to real hard work, the results would come much quicker and there would be fewer broken hearts.

Building a Vocal Repertoire

by

ALMA GLUCK

[Biographical sketch by James Francis Cooke]

[Mme. Alma Gluck was born at Jassy, Roumania. Her father played the violin, but was not a professional musician. At the age of six she was brought to America. She was taught the piano and sang naturally, but had no idea of becoming a singer. Her vocal training was not begun until she was twenty years of age. Her teacher, at that time, was Signor Buzzi-Peccia, with whom she remained for three years, going directly from his studio to the Metropolitan Opera House of New York. She remained there for three years, when the immense success of her concert work drew her away from opera. She then studied with Jean de Reszke, and later with Mme. Sembrich for four or five years. Since then she has appeared in all parts of the United States with unvarying success. Her records have been among the most popular of any ever issued. Together with her husband, Efrem Zimbalist, the distinguished violinist, she has appeared before immense audiences in joint recitals.]

Many seem surprised when I tell them that my vocal training did not begin until I was twenty years of age. It seems to me that it is a very great mistake for any girl to begin the serious study of singing before that age, as the feminine voice, in most instances, is hardly settled until then. Vocal study before that time is likely to be injurious, though some survive it in the hands of very careful and understanding teachers.

The first kind of a repertoire that the student should acquire is a repertoire of solfeggios. I am a great believer in the solfeggio. Using that for a basis, one is assured of acquiring facility and musical accuracy. The experienced listener can tell at once the voice that has had such training. Always remember that musicianship carries one much further than a good natural voice. The voice, even more than the hands, needs a kind of exhaustive technical drill. This is because in this training you are really building the instrument itself. In the piano, one has the instrument complete before he begins; but in the case of the voice, the instrument has to be developed and sometimes *made* by study. When the pupil is practicing, tones grow in volume, richness and fluency.

There are exercises by Bordogni, Concone, Vaccai, Lamperti, Marchesi, Panofka, Panserson and many others with which I am not familiar, which are marvelously beneficial when intelligently studied. These I sang on the syllable "ah," and not with the customary syllable names. It has been said that the syllables Do, Re, Mi, Fa, etc., aid one in reading. To my mind, they are often confusing.

GO TO THE CLASSICS

After a thorough drilling in solfeggios and technical exercises, I would have the student work on the operatic arias of Bellini, Rossini, Donizetti, Verdi, and others. These men knew how to write for the human voice! Their arias are so vocal that the voice develops under them and the student gains vocal assurance. They were written before modern philosophy entered into music—when music was intended for the ear rather than for the mind. I cannot lay too much stress on the importance of using these arias. They are a tonic for the voice, and bring back the elasticity which the more subdued singing of songs taxes.

When one is painting pictures through words, and trying to create atmosphere in songs, so much repression is brought into play that the voice must have a safety-valve, and that one finds in the bravura arias. Here one sings for about fifty bars, "The sky is clouded for me," "I have been betrayed," or "Joy abounds"—the words being simply a vehicle for the ever-moving melody.

When hearing an artist like John McCormack sing a popular ballad it all seems so easy, but in reality songs of that type are the very hardest to sing and must have back of them years of hard training or they fall to banality. They are far more difficult than the limpid operatic arias, and are actually dangerous for the insufficiently trained voice.

THE LYRIC SONG REPERTOIRE

Then when the student has her voice under complete control, it is safe to take up the lyric repertoire of Mendelssohn, Old English Songs, etc.

How simple and charming they are! The works of the lighter French composers, Hahn, Massenet, Chaminade, Gounod, and others. Then Handel, Haydn, Mozart, Löwe, Schubert, Schumann and Brahms. Later the student will continue with Strauss, Wolf, Reger, Rimsky-Korsakoff, Moussorgsky, Borodin and Rachmaninoff. Then the modern French composers, Ravel, Debussy, Georges, Köchlin, Hüe, Chausson, and others. I leave French for the last because it is, in many ways, more difficult for an English-speaking person to sing. It is so full of complex and trying vowels that it requires the utmost subtlety to overcome these difficulties and still retain clarity in diction. For that reason the student should have the advice of a native French coach.

When one has traveled this long road, then he is qualified to sing English songs and ballads.

AMERICAN SONGS

In this country we are rich in the quantity of songs rather than in the quality. The singer has to go through hundreds of compositions before he finds one that really says something. Commercialism overwhelms our composers. They approach their work with the question, "Will this go?" The spirit in which a work is conceived is that in which it will be executed. Inspired by the purse rather than the soul, the mercenary side fairly screams in many of the works put out by every-day American publishers. This does not mean that a song should be queer or ugly to be novel or immortal. It means that the sincerity of the art worker must permeate it as naturally as the green leaves break through the dead branches in springtime. Of the vast number of new American composers, there are hardly more than a dozen who seem to approach their work in the proper spirit of artistic reverence.

ART FOR ART'S SAKE, A FARCE

Nothing annoys me quite so much as the hysterical hypocrites who are forever prating about "art for art's sake." What nonsense! The student who deceives himself into thinking that he is giving his life like an ascetic in the spirit of sacrifice for art is the victim of a deplorable species of egotism. Art for art's sake is just as iniquitous an attitude in its way as art for money's sake. The real artist has no idea that he is sacrificing himself for art. He does what he does for one reason and one reason only—he can't help doing it. Just as the bird sings or the butterfly soars, because it is his natural characteristic, so the artist works.

Time and again a student will send me an urgent appeal to hear her, saying she is poor and wants my advice as to whether it is worth while to continue her studies. I invariably refuse such requests, saying that if the student could give up her work on my advice she had better give it up without it. One does not study for a goal. One sings because one can't help it! The "goal" nine times out of ten is a mere accident.

Art for art's sake is the mask of studio idlers. The task of acquiring a repertoire in these days, when the vocal literature is so immense, is so overwhelming, that the student with sense will devote all his energies to work, and not imagine himself a martyr to art.

🙼

Causation

An interview with
Yeatman Griffith

by Harriette Brower

"The causation of beautiful singing can only be found through a pure and velvety production of the voice, and this is acquired in no other way than by a thorough understanding of what constitutes a perfect beginning— that is the attack or start of the tone. If the tone has a perfect beginning it must surely have a perfect ending."

Thus Mr. Yeatman Griffith began a conference on the subject of vocal technic and the art of song. He had had a day crowded to the brim with work—although all days were usually alike filled—yet he seemed as fresh and unwearied as though the day had only just begun. One felt that here was a man who takes true satisfaction in his work of imparting to others; his work is evidently not a tiresome task but a real joy. Mrs. Griffith shares this joy of work with her husband. "It is most ideal," she says; "we have so grown into it together; we love it."

As is well known, this artist pair returned to their home land at the outbreak of the war, after having resided and taught for five years in London, and previous to that for one year in Florence, Italy. Of course they were both singers, giving recitals together, like the Henschels, and appearing in concert and oratorio. But constant public activity is incompatible with a large teaching practice. One or the other has to suffer. "We chose to do the teaching and sacrifice our public career," said Mr. Griffith. During the five years in which these artists have resided in New York, they have accomplished much; their influence has been an artistic impulse toward the ideals of beautiful singing. Among their many artist pupils who are making names for themselves, it may be mentioned that Florence Macbeth, a charming coloratura soprano, owes much of her success to their careful guidance.

"Michelangelo has said," continued Mr. Griffith, "that 'a perfect start is our first and greatest assurance of a perfect finish.' And nowhere is this precept more truly exemplified than in vocal tone production. The tone must have the right beginning, then it will be right all through. A faulty beginning is to blame for most of the vocal faults and sins of singers. Our country is full of beautiful natural voices; through lack of understanding many of them, even when devoting time and money to study, never become more than mediocre, when they might have developed into really glorious voices if they had only had the right kind of treatment.

TONE PLACEMENT

"We hear a great deal about tone placement in these days; the world seems to have gone mad over the idea. But it is an erroneous idea. How futile to attempt to place the tone in any particular spot in the anatomy. You can focus the tone, but you cannot place it. There is but one place for it to come from and no other place. It is either emitted with artistic effect or it is not. If not, then there is stiffness and contraction, and the trouble ought to be remedied at once.

"Every one agrees that if the vocal instrument were something we could see, our task would be comparatively easy. It is because the instrument is hidden that so many false theories about it have sprung up. One teacher advocates a high, active chest; therefore the chest is held high and rigid, while the abdominal muscles are deprived of the strength they should have. Another advises throwing the abdomen forward; still another squares the shoulders and stiffens the neck. These things do not aid in breath control in the least; on the contrary they induce rigidity which is fatal to easy, natural tone emission.

IN THE BEGINNING

"When the pupil comes to me, we at once establish natural, easy conditions of body and an understanding of the causes which produce good tone. We then begin to work on the vowels. They are the backbone of good singing. When they become controlled, they are then preceded by consonants. Take the first vowel, A; it can be preceded by all the consonants of the alphabet one after another, then each vowel in turn can be treated in the same way. We now have syllables; the next step is to use words. Here is where difficulties sometimes arise for the student. The word becomes perfectly easy to sing if vowels and consonants are properly produced. When they are not, words become obstacles. Correct understanding will quickly obviate this.

BREATH CONTROL

"Breath control is indeed a vital need, but it should not be made a bugbear to be greatly feared. The young student imagines he must inflate the lungs almost to bursting, in order that he may take a breath long enough to sing a phrase. Then, as soon as he opens his lips, he allows half the air he has taken in to escape, before he has uttered a sound. With such a beginning he can only gasp a few notes of the phrase. Or he distends the muscles at the waist to the fullest extent and fancies this is the secret of deep breathing. In short, most students make the breathing and breath control a very difficult matter indeed, when it is, or should be, an act most easy and natural. They do not need the large quantity of breath they imagine they do; for a much smaller amount will suffice to do the work. I tell them, 'Inhale simply and naturally, as though you inhaled the fragrance of a flower. And when you open your lips after this full natural breath, do not let the breath escape; the vocal chords will make the tone, if you understand how to make a perfect start. If the action is correct, the vocal chords will meet; they will not be held apart nor will they crowd each other. Allow the diaphragm and respiratory muscles to do their work, never forcing them; then you will soon learn what breath control in singing means. Remember again, not a particle of breath should be allowed to escape. Every other part of the apparatus must be permitted to do its work, otherwise there will be interference somewhere.'

CAUSATION

"Everything pertaining to the study of vocal technic and the art of singing may be summed up in the one word—causation. A cause underlies every effect. If you do not secure the quality of tone you desire, there must be a reason for it. You evidently do not understand the cause which will produce the effect. That is the reason why singers possessing really beautiful voices produce uneven effects and variable results. They may sing a phrase quite perfectly at one moment. A short time after they may repeat the same phrase in quite a different way and not at all perfectly. One night they will sing very beautifully; the next night you might hardly recognize the voice, so changed would be its quality. This would not be the case if they understood causation. A student, rightly taught, should know the cause for everything he does, how he does thus and so and why he does it. A singer should be able to produce the voice correctly, no matter in what position the role he may be singing may require the head or body to be in. In opera the head or body may be placed in difficult unnatural positions, but these should not interfere with good tone production.

REGISTERS

"I am asked sometimes if I teach registers of the voice. I can say decidedly no, I do not teach registers. The voice should be one and entire, from top to bottom, and should be produced as such, no matter in what part of the voice you sing. Throughout the voice the same instrument is doing the work. So, too, with voices of different caliber, the coloratura, lyric and dramatic. Each and all of these may feel the dramatic spirit of the part, but the lighter quality of the voice may prevent the coloratura from expressing it. The world recognizes the dramatic singer in the size of the voice and of the person. From an artistic point of view, however, there are two ways of looking at the question, since the lyric voice may have vivid dramatic instincts, and may be able to bring them out with equal or even greater intensity than the purely dramatic organ.

VOCAL MASTERY

"Vocal mastery is acquired through correct understanding of what constitutes pure vowel sounds, and such control of the breath as will enable one to convert every atom of breath into singing tone. This establishes correct action of the vocal cords and puts the singer in possession of the various tints of the voice.

"When the diaphragm and respiratory muscles support the breath sufficiently and the vocal cords are permitted to do their work, you produce pure tone. Many singers do not understand these two vital principles. They either sing with too much relaxation of the diaphragm and respiratory muscles, or too much rigidity. Consequently the effort becomes local instead of constitutional, which renders the tone hard and strident and variable to pitch. Again the vocal cords are either forced apart or pinched together, with detriment to tone production.

"The real value of control is lost when we attempt to control the singing instrument and the breath by seeking a place for the tone the singing instrument produces. When the vocal cords are allowed to produce pure vowels, correct action is the result and with proper breath support, vocal mastery can be assured."

A Lesson with a Prima Donna

An interview with
FRIEDA HEMPEL

by Harriette Brower

There is no need to say that Frieda Hempel is one of the most admired artists on the opera and concert stage to-day. Every one knows the fact. Miss Hempel has endeared herself to all through her lovely voice, her use of it, her charm of manner and the sincerity of her art.

It is seven years since Miss Hempel first came to sing at the Metropolitan. America has advanced very greatly in musical appreciation during this period. Miss Hempel herself has grown in artistic stature with each new character she has assumed. This season she has exchanged the opera field for that of the concert room, to the regret of opera patrons and all music lovers, who desired to see her at the Metropolitan. Being so constantly on the wing, it has been extremely difficult to secure a word with the admired artist. Late one afternoon, however, toward the end of her very successful concert season, she was able to devote an hour to a conference with the writer on the principles of vocal art.

How fair, slender and girlish she looked, ensconced among the cushions of a comfortable divan in her music room, with a favorite pet dog nestling at her side.

"And you ask how to master the voice; it seems then, I am to give a vocal lesson," she began, with an arch smile, as she caressed the little creature beside her.

BREATHING

"The very first thing for the singer to consider is breath control; always the breathing—the breathing. She thinks of it morning, noon and night. Even before rising in the morning, she has it on her mind, and may do a few little stunts while still reclining. Then, before beginning her vocal technic in the morning, she goes through a series of breathing exercises. Just what they are is unnecessary to indicate, as each teacher may have his own, or the singer has learned for herself what forms are most beneficial.

VOCAL TECHNIC

"The pianist before the public, or the player who hopes to master the instrument in the future, never thinks of omitting the daily task of scales and exercises; he knows that his chances for success would soon be impaired, even ruined, if he should neglect this important and necessary branch of study.

"It is exactly the same thing with the singer. She cannot afford to do without scales and exercises. If she should, the public would soon find it out. She must be in constant practice in order to produce her tones with smoothness and purity; she must also think whether she is producing them with ease. There should never be any strain, no evidence of effort. Voice production must always seem to be the easiest thing in the world. No audience likes to see painful effort in a singer's face or throat.

VOCAL PRACTICE

"The young singer should always practice with a mirror—do not forget that; she must look pleasant under all circumstances. No one cares to look at a singer who makes faces and grimaces, or scowls when she sings. This applies to any one, young or older. Singing must always seem easy, pleasant, graceful, attractive, winning. This must be the mental concept, and, acted upon, the singer will thus win her audience. I do not mean that one should cultivate a grin when singing; that would be going to the other extreme.

"Let the singer also use a watch when she practices, in order not to overdo. I approve of a good deal of technical study, taken in small doses of ten to fifteen minutes at a time. I myself do about two hours or more, though not all technic; but I make these pauses for rest, so that I am not fatigued. After all, while we must have technic, there is so much more to singing than its technic. Technic is indeed a means to an end, more in the art of song than in almost any other form of art. Technic is the background for expressive singing, and to sing expressively is what every one should be striving for.

WHAT IT MEANS TO BE A SINGER

"A beautiful voice is a gift from heaven, but the cultivation of it rests with its possessor. Here in America, girls do not realize the amount of labor and sacrifice involved, or they might not be so eager to enter upon a career. They are too much taken up with teas, parties and social functions to have sufficient time to devote to vocal study and all that goes with it. There are many other things to study; some piano if possible, languages of course, physical culture and acting, to make the body supple and graceful. I say some piano should be included, at least enough to play accompaniments at sight. But when she has mastered her song or role, she needs an accompanist, for she can never play the music as it should be played while she endeavors to interpret the song as that should be sung. One cannot do complete justice to both at the same time.

"In order to study all the subjects required, the girl with a voice must be willing to give most of her day to the work. This means sacrificing the social side and being willing to throw herself heart and soul into the business of adequately preparing for her career.

AMERICAN VOICES

"I find there are quantities of lovely voices here in America. The quality of the American female voice is beautiful; in no country is it finer, not even in Italy. You have good teachers here, too. Then why are there so few American singers who are properly prepared for a career? Why do we hear of so few who make good and amount to something? If the girl has means and good social connections, she is often not ready to sacrifice social gayeties for the austere life of the student. If she is a poor girl, she frequently cannot afford to take up the subjects necessary for her higher development. Instruction is expensive here, and training for opera almost impossible. The operatic coach requires a goodly fee for his services. And when the girl has prepared several roles where shall she find the opportunity to try them out? Inexperienced singers cannot be accepted at the Metropolitan; that is not the place for them. At the prices charged for seats the management cannot afford to engage any but the very best artists. Until there are more opera houses throughout the country, the American girl will still be obliged to go to Europe for experience and routine. In Europe it is all so much easier. Every little city and town has its own opera house, where regular performances are given and where young singers can try their wings and gain experience. The conductor will often help and coach the singer and never expect a fee for it.

THE YOUNG SINGER BEFORE AN AUDIENCE

"The singer who wishes to make a career in concert should constantly study to do things easily and gracefully. She is gracious in manner, and sings to the people as though it gave her personal pleasure to stand before them. She has a happy expression of countenance; she is simple, unaffected and sincere. More than all this her singing must be filled with sentiment and soul; it must be deeply felt or it will not touch others. Of what use will be the most elaborate technic in the world if there is no soul back of it. So the young singer cultivates this power of expression, which grows with constant effort. The artist has learned to share her gift of song with her audience, and sings straight across into the hearts of her listeners. The less experienced singer profits by her example.

"Shall the singer carry her music in a song recital, is a much discussed question. Many come on with nothing on hand. What then happens? The hands are clasped in supplication, as though praying for help. This attitude becomes somewhat harrowing when held for a whole program. Other singers toy with chain or fan, movements which may be very inappropriate to the sentiment of the song they are singing. For myself I prefer to hold in hand a small book containing the words of my songs, for it seems to be more graceful and less obtrusive than the other ways I have mentioned. I never refer to this little book, as I know the words of my songs backward; I could rise in the middle of the night and go through the program without a glance at words or music, so thoroughly do I know what I am singing. Therefore I do not need the book of words, but I shall always carry it, no matter what the critics may say. And why should not the executive artist reassure himself by having his music with him? It seems to me a pianist would feel so much more certain of himself if he had the notes before him; he of course need not look at them, but their presence would take away the fear that is often an obsession. With the notes at hand he could let himself go, give free reign to fancy, without the terrible anxiety he must often feel.

OPERA OR CONCERT

"People often ask whether I prefer to sing in opera or concert. I always answer, I love both. I enjoy opera for many reasons; I love the concert work, and I am also very fond of oratorio. Of course in the opera I am necessarily restrained; I can never be Frieda Hempel, I must always be some one else; I must always think of the others who are playing with me. In concert I can be myself and express myself. I get near the people; they are my friends and I am theirs. I am much in spirit with oratorio also.

COLORATURA OR DRAMATIC

"Do I think the coloratura voice will ever become dramatic? It depends on the quality of the voice. I think every dramatic singer should cultivate coloratura to some extent—should study smooth legato scales and passages. To listen to some of the dramatic roles of to-day, one would think that smooth legato singing was a lost art. Nothing can take its place, however, and singers should realize this fact."

Miss Hempel believes that every singer, no matter how great, should realize the advantage of constant advice from a capable teacher, in order to prevent the forming of undesirable habits. She also considers that vocal mastery implies the perfection of everything connected with singing; that is to say, perfect breath control, perfect placement of the voice, perfect tone production, together with all requisite grace, feeling and expressiveness.

The Requirements of a Musical Career

An interview with

LOUISE HOMER

by Harriette Brower

Madame Louise Homer is a native artist to whom every loyal American can point with pardonable pride. Her career has been a constant, steady ascent, from the start; it is a career so well known in America that there is hardly any need to review it, except as she herself refers to it on the rare occasions when she is induced to speak of herself. For Mme. Homer is one of the most modest artists in the world; nothing is more distasteful to her than to seek for publicity through ordinary channels. So averse is she to any self-seeking that it was with considerable hesitation that she consented to express her views to the writer, on the singer's art. As Mr. Sidney Homer, the well-known composer and husband of Mme. Homer, remarked, the writer should prize this intimate talk, as it was the first Mme. Homer had granted in a very long time.

The artist had lately returned from a long trip, crowded with many concerts, when I called at the New York residence of this ideal musical pair and their charming family. Mme. Homer was at home and sent down word she would see me shortly. In the few moments of waiting, I seemed to feel the genial atmosphere of this home, its quiet and cheer. A distant tinkle of girlish laughter was borne to me once or twice; then a phrase or two sung by a rich, vibrant voice above; then in a moment after, the artist herself descended and greeted me cordially.

"We will have a cup of tea before we start in to talk," she said, and, as if by magic, the tea tray and dainty muffins appeared.

How wholesome and fresh she looked, with the ruddy color in her cheeks and the firm whiteness of neck and arms. The Japanese robe of "midnight blue," embroidered in yellows, heightened the impression of vigorous health by its becomingness.

FOR THE GIRL WHO WANTS TO MAKE A CAREER

"There is so much to consider for the girl who desires to enter the profession," began Mme. Homer, in response to my first query. "First, she must have a voice, there is no use attempting a career without the voice; there must be something to develop, something worth while to build upon. And if she has the voice and the means to study, she must make up her mind to devote herself exclusively to her art; there is no other way to succeed. She cannot enter society, go to luncheons, dinners and out in the evening, and at the same time accomplish much in the way of musical development. Many girls think, if they attend two or three voice lessons a week and learn some songs and a few operatic arias, that is all there is to it. But there is far more. They must know many other things. The vocal student should study piano and languages; these are really essential. Not that she should strive to become a pianist; that would not be possible if she is destined to become a singer; but the more she knows of the piano and its literature, the more this will cultivate her musical sense and develop her taste.

HOW AN ARTIST WORKS

"I am always studying, always striving to improve what I have already learned and trying to acquire the things I find difficult, or that I have not yet attained to. I do vocal technic every day; this is absolutely essential, while one is in the harness. It is during the winter that I work so industriously, both on technic and repertoire, between tours. This is when I study. I believe in resting the voice part of the year, and I take this rest in the summer. Then, for a time, I do not sing at all. I try to forget there is such a thing as music in the world, so far as studying it is concerned. Of course I try over Mr. Homer's new songs, when they are finished, for summer is his time for composition.

"Since the voice is such an intangible instrument, the singer needs regular guidance and criticism, no matter how advanced she may be. As you say, it is difficult for the singer to determine the full effect of her work; she often thinks it much better than it really is. That is human nature, isn't it?" she added with one of her charming smiles.

THE START IN OPERA

"How did you start upon an operatic career?" the singer was asked.

Just here Mr. Homer entered and joined in the conference.

"I do not desire to go into my life-history, as that would take too long. In a few words, this is how it happened—years ago.

"We were living in Boston; I had a church position, so we were each busy with our musical work. My voice was said to be 'glorious,' but it was a cumbersome, unwieldy organ. I could only sing up to F; there were so many things I wanted to do with my voice that seemed impossible, that I realized I needed more training. I could have remained where I was; the church people were quite satisfied, and I sang in concert whenever opportunity offered. But something within urged me on. We decided to take a year off and spend it in study abroad. Paris was then the Mecca for singers and to Paris we went. I plunged at once into absorbing study; daily lessons in voice training and repertoire; languages, and French diction, several times a week, and soon acting was added, for every one said my voice was for the theater. I had no idea, when I started out, that I should go into opera. I had always loved to sing, as far back as I can remember. My father was a Presbyterian clergyman, and when we needed new hymn books for church or Sunday School, they used to come to our house. I would get hold of every hymn book I could find and learn the music. So I was always singing; but an operatic career never entered my thought, until the prospect seemed to unfold before me, as a result of my arduous study in Paris. Of course I began to learn important arias from the operas. Every contralto aspires to sing the grand air from the last act of *Le Prophète;* you know it of course. I told my teacher I could never do it, as it demanded higher tones than I had acquired, going up to C. He assured me it would be perfectly easy in a little while, if I would spend a few moments daily on those high notes. His prediction was correct, for in a few months I had no trouble with the top notes.

"I studied stage deportment and acting from one of the greatest singing actors of the French stage, Paul Lhérie. What an artist he was! So subtle, so penetrating, so comprehensive. The principles he taught are a constant help to me now, and his remarks often come back to me as I study a new role.

"As I say, I studied this line of work, not knowing what would grow out of it; I did it on faith, hoping that it might prove useful."

"It seems to me," remarked the composer, "that young singers would do well to make a study of acting, along with languages and piano. Then, if the voice developed and an operatic career opened to them, they would be so much better prepared; they would have made a start in the right direction; there would not be so much to learn all at once, later on."

"If the girl could only be sure she was destined for a stage career," said Mme. Homer, thoughtfully, "she might do many things from the start that she doesn't think of doing before she knows.

"To go on with my Paris story. I kept faithfully at work for a year, preparing myself for I knew not just what; I could not guess what was in store. Then I got my first opera engagement, quite unexpectedly. I was singing for some professional friends in a large *salle*. I noticed a man standing with his back to me, looking out of one of the long windows. When I finished, he came forward and offered me an engagement at Vichy, for the summer season. The name Vichy only suggested to my mind a kind of beverage. Now I learned the town had a flourishing opera house, and I was expected to sing eight roles. Thus my stage career began."

What Are the Assets for a Career?

"And what must the girl possess, who wishes to make a success with her singing?" was asked.

"First of all, as I have already said, she must have a voice; she can never expect to get very far without that. Voice is a necessity for a singer, but it rests with her what she will do with it, how she will develop it.

"The next asset is intelligence; that is as great a necessity as a voice. For through the voice we express what we feel, what we are; intelligence controls, directs, shines through and illumines everything. Indeed what can be done without intelligence? I could mention a young singer with a good natural voice, who takes her tones correctly, who studies well; indeed one can find no fault with the technical side of her work; but her singing has no meaning—it says absolutely nothing; it only represents just so many notes."

"That is because she has not a musical nature," put in Mr. Homer. "To my mind that is the greatest asset any one can have who wishes to become a musician in any branch of the art. What can be done without a musical nature? Of course I speak of the young singer who wishes to make a career. There are many young people who take up singing for their own pleasure, never expecting to do much with it. And it is a good thing to do so. It gives pleasure to their family and friends—is a healthful exercise and, last but not least, is financially good for the teacher they employ.

"But the trouble comes when these superficial students aspire to become opera singers after a couple of seasons' study. Of course they all cast eyes at the Metropolitan, as the end and aim of all striving.

"Just as if, when a young man enters a law office, it is going to lead him to the White House, or that he expects it will," said Mr. Homer.

"Then," resumed the artist, "we have already three requirements for a vocal career: voice, intelligence and a musical nature. I think the fourth should be a capacity for work. Without application, the gifts of voice, intelligence and a musical nature will not make an artist. To accomplish this task requires ceaseless labor, without yielding to discouragement. Perhaps the fifth asset would be a cheerful optimism as proof against discouragement.

"That is the last thing the student should yield to—discouragement, for this has stunted or impaired the growth of many singers possessed of natural talent. The young singer must never be down-hearted. Suppose things do not go as she would like to have them; she must learn to overcome obstacles, not be overcome by them. She must have backbone enough to stand up under disappointments; they are the test of her mettle, of her worthiness to enter the circle with those who have overcome. For she can be sure that none of us have risen to a place in art without the hardest kind of work, struggle and the conquering of all sorts of difficulties.

"The sixth asset ought to be patience, for she will need that in large measure. It is only with patient striving, doing the daily vocal task, and trying to do it each day a little better than the day before, that anything worth while is accomplished. It is a work that cannot be hurried. I repeat it; the student must have unlimited patience to labor and wait for results.

Coloratura and Dramatic

"I would advise every student to study coloratura first. Then, as the voice broadens, deepens and takes on a richer timbre, it will turn naturally to the more dramatic expression. The voice needs this background, or foundation in the old Italian music, in order to acquire flexibility and freedom. I was not trained to follow this plan myself, but my daughter Louise, who is just starting out in her public career, has been brought up to this idea, which seems to me the best.

Memorizing

"I memorize very easily, learning both words and music at the same time. In taking up a new role, my accompanist plays it for me and we go over it carefully noting all there is in language and notes. When I can take it to bed with me, and go over it mentally; when I can go through it as I walk along the street, then it has become a part of me; then I can feel I know it."

"Mme. Homer holds the banner at the Metropolitan for rapid memorizing," said her husband. "On one occasion, when *Das Rheingold* was announced for an evening performance, the Fricka was suddenly indisposed and unable to appear. Early in the afternoon, the Director came to Mme. Homer, begging her to do the part, as otherwise he would be forced to close the house that night. A singer had tried all forenoon to learn the role, but had now given it up as impossible. Mme. Homer consented. She started in at three o'clock and worked till six, went on in the evening, sang the part without rehearsal, and acquitted herself with credit. This record has never been surpassed at the Metropolitan."

"I knew the other Frickas of the *Ring*," said Madame, "but had never learned the one in the *Rheingold*; it is full of short phrases and difficult to remember, but I came through all right. I may add, as you ask, that perhaps Orfeo is my favorite role, one of the most beautiful works we have."

VOCAL MASTERY

"What do I understand by 'vocal mastery'? The words explain themselves. The singer must master all difficulties of technic, of tone production, so as to be able to express the thought of the composer, and the meaning of the music."

"Don't forget that the singer must have a musical nature," added Mr. Homer, "for without this true vocal mastery is impossible."

ↄᴓ⊚

A Visit to Mme. Lilli Lehmann

by Harriette Brower

A number of years before the great war, a party of us were spending a few weeks in Berlin. It was midsummer; the city, filled as it was for one of us at least, with dear memories of student days, was in most alluring mood. Flowers bloomed along every balcony, vines festooned themselves from windows and doorways, as well as from many unexpected corners. The parks, large and small, which are the delight of a great city, were at their best and greenest—gay with color. Many profitable hours were spent wandering through the galleries and museums, hearing concerts and opera, and visiting the old quarters of the city, so picturesque and full of memories.

Two of us, who were musicians, were anxious to meet the famous dramatic soprano Lilli Lehmann, who was living quietly in one of the suburbs of the city. Notes were exchanged, and on a certain day we were bidden to come, out of the regular hours for visitors, by "special exception."

How well I remember the drive through the newer residential section of Berlin. The path before long led us through country estates, past beautifully kept gardens and orchards. Our destination was the little suburb of Gruenewald, itself like a big garden, with villas nestling close to each other, usually set back from the quiet, shaded streets. Some of the villas had iron gratings along the pathway, through which one saw gay flowers and garden walks, often statuary and fountains. Other homes were secluded from the street by high brick walls, frequently decorated on top by urns holding flowers and drooping vines.

Behind such a picturesque barrier, we found the gateway which led to Mme. Lehmann's cottage. We rang and soon a trim maid came to undo the iron gate. The few steps leading to the house door did not face us as we entered the inclosure, but led up from the side. We wanted to linger and admire the shrubs and flowering plants, but the maid hastened before us so we had to follow.

From the wide entrance hall doors led into rooms on either hand. We were shown into a salon on the left, and bidden to await Madame's coming.

In the few moments of restful quiet before she entered, we had time to glance over this sanctum of a great artist. To say it was filled with mementos and *objets d'art* hardly expresses the sense of repleteness. Every square foot was occupied by some treasure. Let the eye travel around the room. At the left, as one entered the doorway, stood a fine bust of the artist, chiseled in pure white marble, supported on a pedestal of black marble. Then came three long, French windows, opening into a green garden. Across the farther window stood a grand piano, loaded with music. At the further end of the room, if memory serves, hung a large, full length portrait of the artist herself. A writing desk, laden with souvenirs, stood near. On the opposite side a divan covered with rich brocade; more paintings on the walls, one very large landscape by a celebrated German painter.

Before we could note further details, Mme. Lehmann stood in the doorway, then came forward and greeted us cordially.

How often I had seen her impersonate her great roles, both in Germany and America. They were always of some queenly character. Could it be possible this was the famous Lehmann, this simple housewife, in black skirt and white blouse, with a little apron as badge of home keeping. But there was the stately tread, the grand manner, the graceful movement. What mattered if the silver hair were drawn back severely from the face; there was the dignity of expression, classic features, penetrating glance and mobile mouth I remembered.

After chatting a short time and asking many questions about America, where her experiences had been so pleasant, our talk was interrupted, for a little, by a voice trial, which Madame had agreed to give. Many young singers, from everywhere, were anxious to have expert judgment on their progress or attainments, so Lehmann was often appealed to and gave frequent auditions of this kind. The fee was considerable, but she never kept a penny of it for herself; it all went to one of her favorite charities. The young girl who on this day presented herself for the ordeal was an American, who, it seemed, had not carried her studies very far.

Examining a Pupil

Mme. Lehmann seated herself at the piano and asked for scales and vocalises. The young girl, either from fright or poor training, did not make a very fortunate impression. She could not seem to bring out a single pure steady tone, much less sing scales acceptably.

Madame, with a resigned look, finally asked for a song, which was given. It was a little song of Franz, I remember. Then Lehmann wheeled around on the stool and said to us, in German:

"The girl cannot sing—she has little or no voice to begin with, and has not been rightly trained." Then to the young girl she said, kindly, in English:

"My dear young lady, you have almost everything to learn about singing, for as yet you cannot even sing one tone correctly; you cannot even speak correctly. First of all you need physical development; you must broaden your chest through breathing exercises; you are too thin-chested. You must become physically stronger if you ever hope to sing acceptably. Then you must study diction and languages. This is absolutely necessary for the singer. Above all you must know how to pronounce and sing in your own language. So many do not think it necessary to study their own language; they think they know that already; but one's mother tongue requires study as well as any other language.

"The trouble with American girls is they are always in a hurry. They are not content to sit down quietly and study till they have developed themselves into something before they ever think of coming to Europe. They think if they can just come over here and sing for an artist, that fact alone will give them prestige in America. But that gives them quite the opposite reputation over here. American girls are too often looked upon as superficial, because they come over here quite unprepared. I say to all of them, as I say to you: Go home and study; there are plenty of good teachers of voice and piano in your own land. Then, when you can *sing,* come over here, if you wish; but do not come until you are prepared."

After this little episode, we continued our talk for a while longer. Then, fearing to trespass on her time, we rose to leave. She came to the door with us, followed us down the steps into the front garden, and held the gate open for us, when we finally left. We had already expressed the hope that she might be able to return to America, at no very distant day, and repeat her former triumphs there. Her fine face lighted at the thought, and her last words to us were, as she held open the little iron wicket, "I have a great desire to go to your country again; perhaps, in a year or two—who knows—I may be able to do it."

She stood there, a noble, commanding figure, framed in the green of her garden, and waved her handkerchief, till our cab turned a corner, and she was lost to our view.

THE MOZART FESTIVAL

Several years later, a year before the world war started, to be exact, we had the pleasure of meeting the artist again, and this time, of hearing her sing.

It was the occasion of the Mozart Festival in Salzburg. It is well known that Lehmann, devoted as she has always been to the genius of Mozart, and one of the greatest interpreters of his music, had thrown her whole energy into the founding of a suitable memorial to the master in his native city. This memorial was to consist of a large music school, a concert hall and home for opera. The Mozarteum was not yet completed, but a Festival was held each year in Salzburg, to aid the project. Madame Lehmann was always present and sang on these occasions.

We timed our visit to Mozart's birthplace, so that we should be able to attend the Festival, which lasted as usual five days. The concerts were held in the Aula Academica, a fine *Saal* in the old picturesque quarter of the city.

At the opening concert, Lehmann sang a long, difficult concert aria of Mozart. We could not help wondering, before she began, how time had treated this great organ; whether we should be able to recognize the famous Lehmann who had formerly taken such high rank as singer and interpreter in America. We need not have feared that the voice had become impaired. Or, if it had been, it had become rejuvenated on this occasion. Mme. Lehmann sang with all her well-remembered power and fervor, all her exaltation of spirit, and of course she had a great ovation at the close. She looked like a queen in ivory satin and rare old lace, with jewels on neck, arms and in her silver hair. In the auditorium, three armchairs had been placed in front of the platform. The Archduke, Prince Eugen, the royal patron of the Festival, occupied one. When Madame Lehmann had finished her aria, she stepped down from the platform. The Prince rose at once and went to meet her. She gave him her hand with a graceful curtsey and he led her to the armchair next his own, which had evidently been placed in position for her special use.

At the close of the concert we had a brief chat with her. The next day she was present at the morning concert. This time she was gowned in black, with an ermine cape thrown over her shoulders. The Archduke sat beside her in the armchair, as he had done the evening before. We had a bow and smile as she passed down the aisle.

We trust the Mozarteum in Salzburg, for which Mme. Lehmann has labored with such devotion, will one day fulfill its noble mission.

LEHMANN THE TEACHER

As a teacher of the art of singing, Madame Lehmann has long been a recognized authority, and many artists now actively before the public have come from under her capable hands. Her book, *How to Sing*—rendered in English by Richard Aldrich (Macmillan)—has illumined the path for many a serious student who seeks light on that strange, wonderful, hidden instrument—the voice. Madame Lehmann, by means of many explanations and numerous plates, endeavors to make clear to the young student how to begin and how to proceed in her vocal studies.

BREATHING

On the important subject of breathing she says:

"No one can sing without preparing for it mentally and physically. It is not enough to sing well, one must know how one does it. I practice many breathing exercises without using tone. Breath becomes voice through effort of will and by use of vocal organs. When singing emit the smallest quantity of breath. Vocal chords are breath regulators; relieve them of all overwork.

"At the start a young voice should be taught to begin in the middle and work both ways—that is, up and down. A tone should never be forced. Begin *piano*, make a long crescendo and return to *piano*. Another exercise employs two connecting half tones, using one or two vowels. During practice stand before a mirror, that one may see what one is doing. Practice about one hour daily. Better that amount each day than ten hours one day and none the next. The test will be: do you feel rested and ready for work each morning? If not, you have done too much the day before."

REGISTERS

In regard to registers Madame Lehmann has this to say: "In the formation of the voice no registers should exist or be created. As long as the word is kept in use, registers will not disappear."

PHYSIOLOGY

In spite of the fact there are many drawings and plates illustrating the various organs of head and throat which are used in singing. Madame Lehmann says:

"The singer is often worried about questions of physiology, whereas she need—must—know little about it.

THE NASAL QUALITY

"The singer must have some nasal quality, otherwise the voice sounds colorless and expressionless. We must sing toward the nose—(not necessarily through the nose).

"For many ills of the voice and tone production, I use long, slow scales. They are an infallible cure.

USE OF THE LIPS

"The lips play a large part in producing variety of tone quality. Each vowel, every word can be colored, as by magic, by well controlled play of the lips. When lips are stiff and unresponsive, the singing is colorless. Lips are final resonators, through which tones must pass, and lip movements can be varied in every conceivable manner."

POWER AND VELOCITY

She humorously writes: "Singers without power and velocity are like horses without tails. For velocity, practice figures of five, six, seven and eight notes, first slowly, then faster and faster, up and down."

Common Sense in Training and Preserving the Voice

by

DAME NELLIE MELBA

[Biographical sketch by James Francis Cooke]

[Dame Nellie Melba (stage name for Mrs. Nellie Porter Armstrong, née Mitchell) is described in *Grove's Dictionary* as "the first singer of British birth to attain such an exalted position upon the lyric stage as well as upon the concert platform." Dame Melba was born at Burnley near Melbourne, May 19th, 1861, of Scotch ancestry. She sang at the Town Hall at Richmond when she was six years of age. She studied piano, harmony, composition and violin very thoroughly. At one time she was considered the finest amateur pianist in Melbourne. She also played the church organ in the local church with much success. In 1882 she married Captain Charles Armstrong, son of Sir Andrew Armstrong, Baronet (of Kinds County, Ireland). In 1886 she sang at Queens Hall in London. After studying with Mme. Marchesi for twelve months she made her debut as Gilda (*Rigoletto*) at the Théâtre de la Monnaie in Brussels. Her success was instantaneous. Her London debut was made in *Lucia* in 1888. One year later she made her Parisian debut in Thomas' *Hamlet*.

In 1894 she created the role of Nedda in *I Pagliacci*. Petrograd "went wild" over her in 1892. In 1892 she repeated her successes and in 1893 she began her long series of American triumphs. The fact that her voice, like that of Patti, has remained astonishingly fresh and silvery despite the enormous amount of singing she has done attests better than anything else to the excellence of her method of singing. In the following conference she gives the secret of preserving the voice.]

HOW CAN A GOOD VOICE BE DETECTED?

The young singer's first anxiety is usually to learn whether her voice is sufficiently good to make it worth while to go through the enormous work of preparing herself for the operatic stage. How is she to determine this? Surely not upon the advice of her immediate friends, nor upon that of those to whom she would naturally turn for spiritual advice, medical advice or legal advice. But this is usually just what she does. Because of the honored positions held by her rector, her physician, or her family lawyer, their services are all brought to bear upon her, and after an examination of her musical ability their unskilled opinion is given a weight it obviously does not deserve. The only one to judge is a skilled musician, with good artistic taste and some experience in voice matters. It is sometimes difficult to approach a singing teacher for this advice, as even the most honest could not fail to be somewhat influenced where there is a prospect of a pupil. I do not mean to malign the thousands of worthy teachers, but such a position is a delicate one, and the pupil should avoid consulting with any adviser except one who is absolutely disinterested.

In any event the mere possession of a voice that is sweet and strong by no means indicates that the owner has the additional equipment which the singer must possess. Musical intelligence is quite as great an asset as the possession of a fine voice. By musical intelligence I mean something quite different from general intelligence. People seem to expect that the young person who desires to become a fine pianist or a fine violinist, or a fine composer, should possess certain musical talents. That is, they should experience a certain quickness in grasping musical problems and executing them. The singer, however, by some peculiar popular ruling seems to be exempted from this. No greater mistake could possibly be made. Very few people are musically gifted. When one of these people happens to possess a good voice, great industry, a love for vocal art, physical strength, patience, good sense, good taste and abundant faith in her possibilities, the chances of making a good singer are excellent. I lay great stress upon great determination and good health. I am often obliged to sing one night, then travel a thousand miles to sing the next night. Notwithstanding such journeys, the singer is expected to be in prime condition, look nice, and please a veritable multitude of comparative strangers all expecting wonderful things from her. Do you wonder that I lay stress upon good health?

The youthful training of the singer should be confined quite strictly to that of obtaining a good general and musical education. That is, the vocal training may be safely postponed until the singer is seventeen or eighteen years of age. Of course there have been cases of famous singers who have sung during their childhood, but they are exceptions to all rules. The study of singing demands the direction of an intelligent, well-ordered mind. It is by no means wholly a matter of imitation. In fact, without some cultivation of the taste—that is, the sense of discriminating between what is good and bad—one may imitate with disastrous results.

WHAT WORK SHOULD THE GIRL UNDER EIGHTEEN DO?

I remember well an incident in my own youth. I once went to a concert and heard a much lauded singer render an aria that was in turn vociferously applauded by the audience. This singer possessed a most wonderful tremolo. Every tone went up and down like the teeth of a saw. It was impossible for her to sing a pure even tone without wobbling up and down. But the untrained audience, hungry to applaud anything musical, had cheered the singer despite the tremolo. Consequently I went home and after a few minutes' work I found that it was possible for me to produce a very wonderful tremolo. I went proudly to my teacher and gave an exhibition of my new acquirement. "Who on earth have you been listening to?" exclaimed my teacher. I confessed and was admonished not to imitate.

The voice in childhood is a very delicate organ despite the wear and tear which children give it by unnecessary howling and screaming. More than this, the child-mind is so susceptible to impressions and these impressions become so firmly fixed that the best vocal training for the child should be that of taking the little one to hear great singers. All that the juvenile mind hears is not lost, although much will be forgotten. However, the better part will be unconsciously stowed away in the subconscious mind, to burst forth later in beautiful song through no different process than that by which the little birds store away the song of the older birds. Dealers in singing birds place them in rooms with older and highly developed singing birds to train them. This is not exactly a process of imitation, but rather one of subconscious assimilation. The bird develops his own song later on, but has the advantage of the stored-up impressions of the trained birds.

A GENERAL MUSICAL TRAINING

I have known many singers to fail dismally because they were simply singers. The idea that all the singer needs to know is how to produce tones resonantly and sweetly, how to run scales, make gestures and smile prettily is a perfectly ridiculous one. Success, particularly operatic success, depends upon a knowledge of a great many things. The general education of the singer should be as well rounded as possible. Nothing the singer ever learns in the public schools, or the high schools, is ever lost. History and languages are most important. I studied Italian and French in my childhood and this knowledge was of immense help to me in my later work. When I first went to Paris I had to acquire a colloquial knowledge of the language, but in all cases I found that the drill in French verbs I had gone through virtually saved me years of work. The French pronunciation is extremely difficult to acquire and some are obliged to reside in France for years before a fluent pronunciation can be counted on.

I cannot speak too emphatically upon the necessity for a thorough musical education. A smattering is only an aggravation. Fortunately, my parents saw to it that I was taught the piano, the organ, the violin and thoroughbass. At first it was thought that I would become a professional pianist; and many were good enough to declare that I was the finest amateur pianist in Melbourne. My Scotch-Presbyterian parents would have been horrified if they had had any idea that they were helping me to a career that was in any way related to the footlights. Fortunately, my splendid father, who is now eighty-five years old, has long since recovered from his prejudices and is the proudest of all over my achievements. But I can not be too grateful to him for his great interest in seeing that my early musical training was comprehensive. Aside from giving me a more musicianly insight into my work, it has proved an immense convenience. I can play any score through. I learn all my operas myself. This enables me to form my own conception, that is, to create it, instead of being unconsciously influenced by the tempos and expression of some other individual. The times that I have depended upon a *répétiteur* have been so few that I can hardly remember them. So there, little girl, when you get on your mother's long train and sing to an imaginary audience of thousands, you will do better to run to the keyboard and practice scales or study your études.

THE FIRST VOCAL PRACTICE

The first vocal practice should be very simple. There should be nothing in the way of an exercise that would encourage forcing of any kind. In fact the young singer should always avoid doing anything beyond the normal.

Remember that a sick body means a sick voice. Again, don't forget your daily outdoor exercise. Horseback riding, golf and tennis are my favorites. An hour's walk on a lovely country road is as good for a singer as an hour's practice. I mean that.

In avoiding strain the pupil must above all things learn to sing the upper notes without effort or rather strain. While it is desirable that a pupil should practice all her notes every day, she should begin with the lower notes, then take the middle notes and then the so-called upper notes or head notes which are generally described as beginning with the F sharp on the top line of the treble staff. This line may be regarded as a danger line for singers young and old. It is imperative that when the soprano sings her head notes, beginning with F sharp and upward, they shall proceed very softly and entirely without strain as they ascend. I can not emphasize this too strongly.

PRESERVING THE VOICE

Let me give you one of my greatest secrets. Like all secrets, it is perfectly simple and entirely rational. *Never give the public all you have.* That is, the singer owes it to herself never to go beyond the boundaries of her vocal possibilities. The singer who sings to the utmost every time is like the athlete who exhausts himself to the state of collapse. This is the only way in which I can account for what the critics term "the remarkable preservation" of my own voice. I have been singing for years in all parts of the musical world, growing richer in musical and human experience and yet my voice to-day feels as fresh and as clear as when I was in my teens. I have never strained, I have never continued roles that proved unsuited to me, I have never sung when I have not been in good voice.

This leads to another very important point. I have often had students ask me how they can determine whether their teachers are giving them the kind of method or instruction they should have. I have always replied, "If you feel tired after a lesson, if your throat is strained after a little singing, if you feel exhausted, your teacher is on the wrong track, no matter what he labels his method or how wonderful his credentials are."

Isn't that very simple? I have known young girls to go on practicing until they couldn't speak. Let them go to a physician and have the doctor show them by means of a laryngoscope just how tender and delicate their vocal organs are. I call them my "little bits of cotton"; they seem so frail and so tiny. Do you wonder that I guard them carefully? This practice consists of the simplest imaginable exercises—sustained scales, chromatic scales and trills. It is not so much *what* one practices, but *how* one practices.

IS THE ART OF SINGING DYING OUT?

We continually hear critics complain that the art of singing is dying. It is easy enough to be a pessimist, and I do not want to class myself with the pessimists; but I can safely say that, unless more attention is paid to the real art of singing, there must be a decadence in a short time. By this I mean that the voice seems to demand a kind of exercise leading to flexibility and fluent tone production that is not found in the ultra-dramatic music of any of the modern composers. Young singers begin with good voices and, after an altogether inadequate term of preparation, they essay the works of Strauss and Wagner. In two years the first sign of a breakup occurs. Their voices become rough—the velvet vanishes and note after note "breaks" disagreeably. The music of the older Italian composers, from Scarlatti or Carissimi to Donizetti and Bellini, despite the absurd libretti of their operas, demanded first of all dulcet tones and limpid fluency. The singers who turned their noses up at the florid arabesques of old Italy for the more rugged pageantry of modern Germany are destined to suffer the consequences. Let us have the masterpieces of the heroic Teutons, by all means, but let them be sung by vocalists trained as vocalists and not merely by actors who have only taken a few steps in vocal art.

The main point of all operatic work must be observed if opera is to continue successfully. Delibes chose me to sing a performance of his *Lakmé* at Brussels. It was to be my debut in French. I had not then mastered the French pronunciation so that I could sing acceptably at the Paris Grand Opera, the scene of my later triumphs. Consequently I was permitted to sing in Brussels. There the directors objected to my pronunciation, calling it "abominable." Delibes replied, *"Qu'elle chante en chinois, si elle veut, mais qu'elle chante mon opéra"* ("Even if she sang in Chinese, I would be glad to have her sing my opera").

I am asked what has been my greatest incentive. I can think of nothing greater than opposition. The early opposition from my family made me more and more determined to prove to them that I would be successful. If I heard some singer who sang successfully the roles I essayed, then I would immediately make up my mind to excel that singer. This is a human trait I know; but I always profited by it. Never be afraid of competition or opposition. The more you overcome, the greater will be your ultimate triumph.

A Child of the Opera

An interview with
CLAUDIA MUZIO

by Harriette Brower

In tales of romance one reads sometimes of a gifted girl who lives in a musical atmosphere all her life, imbibing artistic influences as naturally and almost as unconsciously as the air she breathes. At the right moment, she suddenly comes out into the light and blossoms into a full-fledged singer, to the surprise and wonder of all her friends. Or she is brought up behind the scenes in some great opera house of the world, where, all unnoticed by her elders, she lives in a dream world of her own, peopled by the various characters in the operas to which she daily listens. She watches the stage so closely and constantly that she unconsciously commits the roles of the heroines she most admires to memory. She knows what they sing, how they act the various parts, how they impersonate the characters. Again, at the right moment, the leading prima donna is indisposed, there is no one to take her place; manager is in despair, when the slip of a girl, who is known to have a voice, but has never sung in opera, offers to go on in place of the absent one. She is finally permitted to do so; result, a popular success.

Some pages of Claudia Muzio's musical story read like the romantic experiences of a novel-heroine. She, too, was brought up in great opera houses, and it seemed natural, that in due course of time, she should come into her own, in the greatest lyric theater of the land of her adoption.

When she returned to America, a couple of years ago, after gaining experience in Europe, she arrived toward the end of the season preceding her scheduled debut here, to prepare herself more fully for the coming appearance awaiting her.

I was asked to meet and talk with the young singer, to ascertain her manner of study, and some of her ideas regarding the work which lay before her.

"It was always my dream to sing at the Metropolitan, and my dream has come true."

Claudia Muzio said the words with her brilliant smile, as her great soft dark eyes gazed luminously at the visitor.

The day was cold and dreary without, but the singer's apartment was of tropical warmth. A great bowl of violets on the piano exhaled delicious fragrance; the young Italian in the bloom of her oriental beauty seemed like some luxuriant tropical blossom herself.

Claudia Muzio, who was just about to take her place among the personnel of the Metropolitan, is truly to the manner born—a real child of the opera. She has lived in opera all her life, has imbibed the operatic atmosphere from her earliest remembrance. It must be as necessary for a singer who aspires to fill a high place in this field of artistic endeavor, to live amid congenial surroundings, as for a pianist, violinist or composer to be environed by musical influences.

"Yes, I am an Italian," she began, "for I was born in Italy; but when I was two years old I was taken to London, and my childhood was passed in that great city. My father was stage manager at Covent Garden, and has also held the same post at the Manhattan and Metropolitan Opera Houses in New York. So I have grown up in the theater. I have always listened to opera—daily, and my childish imagination was fired by seeing the art of the great singers. I always hoped I should one day become a singer, so I always watched the artists in action, noting how they did everything. As a result, I do not now have to study acting as a separate branch of the work, for acting comes to me naturally. I am very temperamental; I feel intuitively how the role should be enacted.

"All tiny children learn to sing little songs, and I was no exception. I acquired quite a number, and at the age of six exhibited my accomplishments at a little recital. But I never had singing lessons until I began to study seriously at about the age of sixteen. Although I did not study the voice till I reached that age, I was always occupied with music, for I learned as a little girl to play both harp and piano.

"We lived in London, of which city I am very fond, from the time I was two, till I was fourteen, then we came to America. After residing here a couple of years, it was decided I should make a career, and we went to Italy. I was taken to Madame Anna Casaloni at Turino. She was quite elderly at that time, but she had been a great singer. When she tried my voice, she told me it was quite properly placed—so I had none of that drudgery to go through.

"At first my voice was a very light soprano, hardly yet a coloratura. It became so a little later, however, and then gradually developed into a dramatic soprano. I am very happy about this fact, for I love to portray tears as well as laughter—sorrow and tragedy as well as lightness and gayety. The coloratura manner of singing is all delicacy and lightness, and one cannot express deep emotion in this way.

"We subsequently went to Milano, where I studied with Madame Viviani, a soprano who had enjoyed great success on the operatic stage.

"After several years of serious study I was ready to begin my career. So I sang in Milan and other Italian cities, then at Covent Garden, and now I am in the Metropolitan. In Italy I created the role of Fiora in *Amore dei*

Tre Re, and sang with Ferrari-Fontana. I also created Francesca in *Francesca da Rimini,* under its composer, Zandonai. I have a repertoire of about thirty operas, and am of course adding to it constantly, as one must know many more than thirty roles. Since coming to New York, I have learned *Aïda,* which I did not know before, and have already appeared in it. It was learned thoroughly in eight days. Now I am at work on *Madame Butterfly.*

TECHNICAL PRACTICE

"I work regularly every morning on vocal technic. Not necessarily a whole hour at a stretch, as some do; but as much time as I feel I need. I give practically my whole day to study, so that I can make frequent short pauses in technical practice. If technic is studied with complete concentration and vigor, as it always should be, it is much more fatiguing than singing an opera role.

"You ask about the special forms of exercises I use. I sing all the scales, one octave each—once slow and once fast—all in one breath. Then I sing triplets on each tone, as many as I can in one breath. I can sing about fifteen now, but I shall doubtless increase the number. For all these I use full power of tone. Another form of exercise is to take one tone softly, then go to the octave above, which tone is also sung softly, but there is a large crescendo made between the two soft tones. My compass is three octaves— from C below middle C to two octaves above that point. I also have C sharp, but I do not practice it, for I know I can reach it if I need it, and I save my voice. Neither do I work on the final tones of the lowest octave, for the same reason—to preserve the voice.

BREATH CONTROL

"Every singer knows how important is the management of the breath. I always hold the chest up, taking as long breaths as I can conveniently do. The power to hold the breath, and sing more and more tones with one breath, grows with careful, intelligent practice. There are no rules about the number of phrases you can sing with a single breath. A teacher will tell you; if you can sing two phrases with one breath, do so; if not, take breath between. It all rests with the singer.

MEMORIZING

"I learn words and music of a role at the same time, for one helps the other. When I have mastered a role, I know it absolutely, words, music and accompaniment. I can always play my accompaniments, for I understand the piano. I am always at work on repertoire, even at night. I don't seem to need very much sleep, I think, and I often memorize during the night; that is such a good time to work, for all is so quiet and still. I lie awake thinking of the music, and in this way I learn it. Or, perhaps it learns itself. For when I retire the music is not yet mastered, not yet my own, but when morning comes I really know it.

"Of course I must know the words with great exactness, especially in songs. I shall do English songs in my coming song recital work, and the words and diction must be perfect, or people will criticize my English. I always write out the words of my roles, so as to be sure I understand them and have them correctly memorized.

KEEPING UP REPERTOIRE

"Most singers, I believe, need a couple of days—sometimes longer—in which to review a role. I never use the notes or score when going over a part in which I have appeared, for I know them absolutely, so there is no occasion to use the notes. Other singers appear frequently at rehearsal with their books, but I never take mine. My intimate knowledge of score, when I assisted my father in taking charge of operatic scores, is always a great help to me. I used to take charge of all the scores for him, and knew all the cuts, changes and just how they were to be used. The singers themselves often came to me for stage directions about their parts, knowing I had this experience.

"Yes, as you suggest, I could sing here in winter, then in South America in summer." (Miss Muzio accomplished this recently, with distinguished success and had many thrilling adventures incident to travel.) "This would mean I would have no summer at all, for that season with them is colder than we have it here. No, I want my summer for rest and study. During the season at the Metropolitan I give up everything for my art. I refuse all society and the many invitations I receive to be guest of honor here and there. I remain quietly at home, steadfastly at work. My art means everything to me, and I must keep myself in the best condition possible, to be ready when the call comes to sing. One cannot do both, you know; art and society do not mix well. I have never disappointed an audience; it would be a great calamity to be obliged to do so."

Patience and Perseverance Win Results

An interview with

ROSA RAISA

by Harriette Brower

To the present-day opera-goers the name of Rosa Raisa stands for a compelling force. In whatever role she appears, she is always a commanding figure, both physically, dramatically and musically. Her feeling for dramatic climax, the intensity with which she projects each character assumed, the sincerity and self-forgetfulness of her naturalistic interpretation, make every role notable. Her voice is a rich, powerful soprano, vibrantly sweet when at its softest—like a rushing torrent of passion in intense moments. At such moments the listener is impressed with the belief that power and depth of tone are limitless; that the singer can never come to the end of her resources, no matter how deeply she may draw on them. There are such moments of tragic intensity, in her impersonation of the heroine in *Jewels of the Madonna,* in *Sister Angelica,* in *Norma,* as the avenging priestess, in which role she has recently created such a remarkable impression.

A PRIMA DONNA AT HOME

If one has pictured to one's self that because the Russian prima donna can show herself a whirlwind of dynamic passion on the stage, therefore she must show some of these qualities in private life, one would quickly become disabused of such an impression when face to face with the artist. One would then meet a slender, graceful young woman, of gentle presence and with the simplest manners in the world. The dark, liquid eyes look at one with frankness and sincerity; the wide, low brow, from which the dark hair is softly drawn away, is the brow of a madonna. In repose the features might easily belong to one of Raphael's saints. However, they light up genially when their owner speaks.

Mme. Raisa stood in the doorway of her New York apartment, ready to greet us as we were shown the way to her. Her figure, clad in close-fitting black velvet, looked especially slender; her manner was kind and gracious and we were soon seated in her large, comfortable salon, deep in conference. Before we had really begun, the singer's pet dog came bounding to greet us from another room. The tiny creature, a Mexican terrier, was most affectionate, yet very gentle withal, and content to quietly cuddle down and listen to the conversation.

"I will speak somewhat softly," began Mme. Raisa, "since speaking seems to tire me much more than singing, for what reason I do not know. We singers must think a little of our physical well being, you see. This means keeping regular hours, living very simply and taking a moderate amount of exercise.

"Yes, I always loved to sing; even as a little child I was constantly singing. And so I began to have singing lessons when I was eight years old. Later on I went to Italy and lived there for a number of years, until I began to travel. I now make my home in Naples. My teacher there was Madame Marchesio, who was a remarkable singer, musician and teacher—all three. Even when she reached the advanced age of eighty, she could still sing wonderfully well. She had the real *bel canto*, understood the voice, how to use it and the best way to preserve it. I owe so much to her careful, artistic training; almost everything, I may say.

THE SINGER'S LIFE

"One cannot expect to succeed in the profession of music without giving one's best time and thought to the work of vocal training and all the other subjects that go with it. A man in business gives his day, or the most of it, to his office. My time is devoted to my art, and indeed I have not any too much time to study all the necessary sides of it.

"During the season, I do regular vocal practice each day and keep the various roles in review. During the summer I study new parts, for then I have the time and the quiet. That is what the singer needs—quiet. I always return to Naples for the vacation, unless I go to South America and sing there. Then I must have a little rest too, that I may be ready for the labors of the following season.

VOCAL TRAINING

"Even during the busiest days technic practice is never neglected. Vocalises, scales, terzetta—what you call them—broken thirds, yes, and long, slow tones in *messa di voce*, that is, beginning softly, swelling to loud then gradually diminishing to soft, are part of the daily regime. One cannot omit these things if one would always keep in condition and readiness. When at work in daily study, I sing softly, or with medium tone quality; I do not use full voice except occasionally, when I am going through a part and wish to try out certain effects.

"ONE VOICE"

"I was trained first as a coloratura and taught to do all the old Italian operas of Bellini, Rossini, Donizetti and the rest of the florid Italian school. This gives the singer a thorough, solid training—the sort of training that requires eight or ten years to accomplish. But this is not too much time to give, if one wishes to be thoroughly prepared to sing all styles of music. In former days, when singers realized the necessity of being prepared in this way, there existed I might say—*one voice;* for the soprano voice was trained to sing both florid and dramatic music. But in these days sopranos are divided into High, Lyric, Coloratura and Dramatic; singers choose which of these lines seems to suit best their voice and temperament.

Coloratura and Dramatic

"It is of advantage to the singer to be trained in both these arts. In the smaller opera houses of Italy, a soprano, if thus trained, can sing *Lucia* one night and *Norma* the next; *Traviata* one night and *Trovatore* the next.

"Modern Italian opera calls for the dramatic soprano. She must be an actress just as well as a singer. She must be able to express in both voice and gesture intense passion and emotion. It is the period of storm and stress. Coloratura voices have not so much opportunity at the present time, unless they are quite out of the ordinary. And yet, for me, a singer who has mastery of the beautiful art of *bel canto* is a great joy. Galli-Curci's art is the highest I know of. For me she is the greatest singer. Melba also is wonderful. I have heard her often—she has been very kind to me. When I hear her sing an old Italian air, with those pure, bell-like tones of hers, I am lifted far up; I feel myself above the sky.

Do Not Yield to Discouragement

"The younger singer need not yield to discouragement, for she must know from the start that the mastery of a great art like singing is a long and arduous task. If the work seems too difficult at times, do not give up or say 'I cannot.' If I had done that, I should have really given up many times. Instead I say: 'I can do it, and not only I can but I will!'

Musicianship

"There are so many sides to the singer's equipment, besides singing itself"; and Mme. Raisa lifted dark eyes and spread out her graceful hands as though to indicate the bigness of the subject. "Yes, there is the piano, for instance; the singer is much handicapped without a knowledge of that instrument, for it not only provides accompaniment but cultivates the musical sense. Of course I have learned the piano and I consider it necessary for the singer.

"Then there are languages. Be not content with your own, though that language must be perfectly learned and expressed, but learn others."

"You of course speak several languages?" questioned the listener.

"Yes, I speak eight," she answered modestly. "Russian, of course, for I am Russian; then French, Italian, German, Spanish, Polish, Roumanian and English. Besides these I am familiar with a few dialects.

Have Patience

"So many young singers are so impatient; they want to prepare themselves in three or four years for a career," and Madame frowned her disapproval. "Perhaps they may come before the public after that length of time spent in study; but they will only know a part—a little of all they ought to know. With a longer time, conscientiously used, they would be far better equipped. The singer who spends nine or ten years in preparation, who is trained to sing florid parts as well as those which are dramatic—she indeed can sing anything, the music of the old school as well as of the new. In Rome I gave a recital of old music, assisted by members of the Sistine Chapel choir. We gave much old music, some of it dating from the sixth century.

"Do I always feel the emotions I express when singing a role? Yes, I can say that I endeavor to throw myself absolutely into the part I am portraying; but that I always do so with equal success cannot be expected. So many unforeseen occurrences may interfere, which the audience can never know or consider. One may not be exactly in the mood, or in the best of voice; the house may not be a congenial space, or the audience is unsympathetic. But if all is propitious and the audience with you—then you are lifted up and carry every one with you. Then you are inspired and petty annoyances are quite forgotten.

Vocal Mastery

"You ask a very difficult question when you ask of what vocal mastery consists. If I have developed perfect control throughout the two and a half octaves of my voice, can make each tone with pure quality and perfect evenness in the different degrees of loud and soft, and if I have perfect breath control as well, I then have an equipment that may serve all purposes of interpretation.

"Together with vocal mastery must go the art of interpretation, in which all the mastery of the vocal equipment may find expression. In order to interpret adequately one ought to possess a perfect instrument, perfectly trained. When this is the case one can forget mechanism, confident of the ability to express whatever emotion is desired."

"Have you a message which may be carried to the young singers?" she was asked.

"Tell them to have patience—patience to work and patience to wait for results. Vocal mastery is not a thing that can be quickly accomplished; it is not the work of weeks and months, but of years of consistent, constant effort. It cannot be hurried, but must grow with one's growth, both mentally and physically. But the reward of earnest effort is sure to come!"

Keeping the Voice in Prime Condition

by

ERNESTINE SCHUMANN-HEINK

[Biographical sketch by James Francis Cooke]

[Mme. Ernestine Schumann-Heink (née Roessler) was born near the city of Prague, July 15, 1861. She relates that her father was a Czech and her mother was of Italian extraction. She was educated in Ursuline Convent and studied singing with Mme. Marietta von Leclair in Graz. Her first appearance was at the age of 15, when she is reported to have taken a solo part in a performance of the Beethoven Ninth Symphony, at an important concert in Graz. Her operatic debut was made at the Royal Opera, Dresden, in *Trovatore*. There she studied under Krebs and Franz Wüllner. It is impossible to detail Mme. Schumann-Heink's operatic successes here, since her numerous appearances at the leading operatic houses of the world have been followed by such triumphs that she is admittedly the greatest contralto soloist of her time. At Bayreuth, Covent Garden, and at the Metropolitan her appearances have drawn multitudes. In concert she proved one of the greatest of all singers of art songs. In 1905 she became an American citizen, her enthusiasm for this country leading her to name one of her sons George Washington. During the great war (in which four of her sons served with the American colors) she toured incessantly from camp to camp, giving her services for the entertainment of the soldiers and winning countless admirers in this way. Her glorious voice extends from D on the third line of the bass clef to C on the second leger line above the treble clef.]

THE ARTIST'S RESPONSIBILITY

Would you have me give the secret of my success at the very outstart? It is very simple and centers around this subject of the artist's responsibility to the audience. My secret is absolute devotion to the audience. I love my audiences. They are all my friends. I feel a bond with them the moment I step before them. Whether I am singing in blasé New York or before an audience of farmer folk in some Western Chautauqua, my attitude toward my audience is quite the same. I take the same care and thought with every audience. This even extends to my dress. The singer who wears an elaborate gown before a Metropolitan audience and wears some worn-out old rag of a thing when singing at some rural festival, shows that she has not the proper respect in her mind. Respect is everything.

Therefore it is necessary for me to have my voice in the best of condition every day of the year. It is my duty to my audience. The woman who comes to a country Chautauqua and brings her baby with her and perchance nurses the little one during the concert gets a great deal closer to my heart than the stiff-backed aristocrat who has just left a Pekingese spaniel outside of the opera house door in a $6000.00 limousine. That little country woman expects to hear the singer at her best. Therefore, I practice just as carefully on the day of the Chautauqua concert as I would if I were to sing Ortrud the same night at the Metropolitan in New York.

American audiences are becoming more and more discriminating. Likewise they are more and more responsive. As an American citizen, I am devoted to all the ideals of the New World. They have accepted me in the most whole-souled manner and I am grateful to the land of my adoption.

The Advantage of an Early Training

Whether or not the voice keeps in prime condition to-day depends largely upon the early training of the singer. If that training is a good one, a sound one, a sensible one, the voice will, with regular practice, keep in good condition for a remarkably long time. The trouble is that the average student is too impatient in these days to take time for a sufficient training. The voice at the outstart must be trained lightly and carefully. There must not be the least strain. I believe that at the beginning two lessons a week should be sufficient. The lessons should not be longer than one-half an hour and the home practice should not exceed at the start fifty minutes a day. Even then the practice should be divided into two periods. The young singer should practice *mezza voce,* which simply means nothing more or less than "half voice." Never practice with full voice unless singing under the direction of a well-schooled teacher with years of practical singing experience.

It is easy enough to shout. Some of the singers in modern opera seem to employ a kind of megaphone method. They stand stock still on the stage and bawl out the phrases as though they were announcing trains in a railroad terminal. Such singers disappear in a few years. Their voices seem torn to shreds. The reason is that they have not given sufficient attention to *bel canto* in their early training. They seem to forget that voice must first of all be beautiful. *Bel canto*—beautiful singing—not the singing of meaningless Italian phrases, as so many insist, but the glorious *bel canto* which Bach, Haydn and Mozart demand—a *bel canto* that cultivates the musical taste, disciplines the voice and trains the singer technically to do great things. Please understand that I am not disparaging the good and beautiful in Italian masterpieces. The musician will know what I mean. The singer can gain little, however, from music that intellectually and vocally is better suited to a parrot than a human being.

Some of the older singers made *bel canto* such an art that people came to hear them for their voices alone, and not for their intellectual or emotional interpretations of a role. Perhaps you never heard Patti in her prime. Ah! Patti—the wonderful Adelina with the glorious golden voice. It was she who made me ambitious to study breathing until it became an art. To hear her as she trippingly left the stage in Verdi's *Traviata* singing runs with ease and finish that other singers slur or stumble over—ah! that was an art!

il   mio pen - sier, il   mio pen-

sier_____ il   mio   pen - sier.

Volumes have been written on breathing and volumes more could be written. This is not the place to discuss the singer's great fundamental need. Need I say more than that I practice deep breathing every day of my life?

The Age for Starting

It is my opinion that no girl who wishes to keep her voice in the prime of condition all the time in after years should start to study much earlier than seventeen or eighteen years of age. In the case of a man I do not believe that he should start until he is past twenty or even twenty-two. I know that this is contrary to what many singers think, but the period of mutation in both sexes is a much slower process than most teachers realize, and I have given this matter a great deal of serious thought.

LET EVERYBODY SING!

Can I digress long enough to say that I think that everybody should sing? That is, they should learn to sing under a good singing instructor. This does not mean that they should look forward toward a professional career. God forbid! There are enough half-baked singers in the world now who are striving to become professionals. But the public should know that singing is the healthiest kind of exercise imaginable. When one sings properly one exercises nearly all of the important muscles of the torso. The circulation of the blood is improved, the digestion bettered, the heart promoted to healthy action—in fact, everything is bettered. Singers as a rule are notoriously healthy and often very long lived. The new movement for community singing in the open air is a magnificent one. Let everybody sing!

A great singing teacher with a reputation as big as Napoleon's or George Washington's is not needed. There are thousands and thousands of unknown teachers who are most excellent. Often the advice or the instruction is very much the same. What difference does it make whether I buy Castile soap in a huge Broadway store or a little country store, if the soap is the same? Many people hesitate to study because they can not study with a great teacher. Nonsense! Pick out some sensible, well-drilled teacher and then use your own good judgment to guide yourself. Remember that Schumann-Heink did not study with a world-famed teacher. Whoever hears of Marietta von Leclair in these days? Yet I do not think that I could have done any more with my voice if I had had every famous teacher from Nicola Antonio Porpora down to the present day. The individual singer must have ideals, and then leave nothing undone to attain those ideals. One of my ideals was to be able to sing pianissimo with the kind of resonance that makes it carry up to the farthest gallery. That is one of the most difficult things I had to learn, and I attained it only after years of faithful practice.

THE SINGER'S DAILY ROUTINE

To keep the voice in prime condition the singer's first consideration is physical and mental health. If the body or the mind is over-taxed singing becomes an impossibility. It is amazing what the healthy body and the busy mind can really stand. I take but three weeks' vacation during the year and find that I am a great deal better for it. Long terms of enforced indolence do not mean rest. The real artist is happiest when at work, and I want to work. Fortunately I am never at loss for opportunity. The ambitious vocal student can benefit as much by studying a good book on hygiene or the conservation of the health as from a book on the art of singing.

First of all comes diet. Americans as a rule eat far too much. Why do some of the good churchgoing people raise such an incessant row about over-drinking when they constantly injure themselves quite as much by over-eating? What difference does it make whether you ruin your stomach, liver or kidneys by too much alcohol or too much roast beef? One vice is as bad as another. The singer must live upon a light diet. A heavy diet is by no means necessary to keep up a robust physique. I am rarely ill, am exceedingly strong in every way, and yet eat very little indeed. I find that my voice is in the best of condition when I eat very moderately. My digestion is a serious matter with me, and I take every precaution to see that it is not congested in any way. This is most important to the singer. Here is an average menu for my days when I am on tour:

BREAKFAST
Two or more glasses of Cold Water
(not ice water)
Ham and Eggs
Coffee
Toast.

MID-DAY DINNER
Soup
Some Meat Order
A Vegetable
Plenty of Salad
Fruit.

SUPPER
A Sandwich
Fruit.

Such a menu I find ample for the heaviest kind of professional work. If I eat more, my work may deteriorate, and I know it.

Fresh air, sunshine, sufficient rest and daily baths in tepid water night and morning are a part of my regular routine. I lay special stress upon the baths. Nothing invigorates the singer as much as this. Avoid very cold baths, but see to it that you have a good reaction after each bath. There is nothing like such a routine as this to avoid colds. If you have a cold try the same remedies to try to get rid of it. To me, one day at Atlantic City is better for a cold than all the medicine I can take. I call Atlantic City my cold doctor. Of course, there are many other shore resorts that may be just as helpful, but when I can do so I always make a bee line for Atlantic City the moment I feel a serious cold on the way.

Sensible singers know now that they must avoid alcohol, even in limited quantities, if they desire to be in the prime of condition and keep the voice for a long, long time. Champagne particularly is poison to the singer just before singing. It seems to irritate the throat and make good vocal work impossible. I am sorry for the singer who feels that some spur like champagne or a cup of strong coffee is desirable before going upon the stage.

It amuses me to hear girls say, "I would give anything to be a great singer"; and then go and lace themselves until they look like Jersey mosquitoes. The breath is the motive power of the voice. Without it under intelligent control nothing can be accomplished. One might as well try to run an automobile without gasoline as sing without breath. How can a girl breathe when she has squeezed her lungs to one-half their normal size?

PREPARATION FOR HEAVY ROLES

The voice can never be kept in prime condition if it is obliged to carry a load that it has not been prepared to carry. Most voices that wear out are voices that have been overburdened. Either the singer does not know how to sing or the role is too heavy. I think that I may be forgiven for pointing out that I have repeatedly sung the heaviest and most exacting roles in opera. My voice would have been shattered years ago if I had not prepared myself for these roles and sung them properly. A man may be able to carry a load of fifty pounds for miles if he carries it on his back, but he will not be able to carry it a quarter of a mile if he holds it out at arm's length from the body, with one arm. Does this not make the point clear?

Some roles demand maturity. It is suicidal for the young singer to attempt them. The composer and the conductor naturally think only of the effect at the performance. The singer's welfare with them is a secondary consideration. I have sung under the great composers and conductors, from Richard Wagner to Richard Strauss. Some of the Strauss roles are even more strenuous than those of Wagner. They call for great energy as well as great vocal ability. Young singers essay these heavy roles and the voices go to pieces. Why not wait a little while? Why not be patient?

The singer is haunted by the delusion that success can only come to her if she sings great roles. If she can not ape Melba in *Traviata,* Emma Eames as Elizabeth in *Tannhäuser* or Geraldine Farrar in *Butterfly,* she pouts and refuses to do anything. Offer her a small part and she sneers at it. Ha! Ha! All my earliest successes were made in the smallest kinds of parts. I realized that I had only a little to do and only very little time to do it in. Consequently, I gave myself heart and soul to that part. It must be done so artistically, so intelligently, so beautifully that it would command success. Imagine the roles of Erda and Norna,* and Marie in *Flying Dutchman*. They are so small that they can hardly be seen. Yet these roles were my first door to success and fame. Wagner did not think of them as little things. He was a real master and knew that in every art-work a small part is just as important as a great part. It is a part of a beautiful whole. Don't turn up your nose at little things. Take every opportunity, and treat it as though it were the greatest thing in your life. It pays.

Everything that amounts to anything in my entire career has come through struggle. At first a horrible struggle with poverty. No girl student in a hall bedroom to-day (and my heart goes out to them now) endures more than I went through. It was work, work, work, from morning to night, with domestic cares and worries enough all the time to drive a woman mad. Keep up your spirits, girls. If you have the right kind of fight in you, success will surely come. Never think of discouragement, no matter what happens. Keep working every day and always hoping. It will come out all right if you have the gift and the perseverance. Compulsion is the greatest element in the vocalist's success. Poverty has a knout in its hand driving you on. Well, let it—and remember that under that knout you will travel twice as fast as the rich girl possibly can with her fifty-horse-power automobile. Keep true to the best *Muss*—"I MUST," "I will," the mere necessity is a help, not a hindrance, if you have the right stuff in you. Learn to depend upon yourself, and know that when you have something that the public wants it will not be slow in running after you. Don't ask for help. I never had any help. Tell that to the aspiring geese who think that I have some magic power whereby I can help a mediocre singer to success by the mere twist of the hand.

Daily Exercises of a Prima Donna

Daily vocal exercises are the daily bread of the singer. They should be practiced just as regularly as one sits down to the table to eat, or as one washes one's teeth or as one bathes. As a rule the average professional singer does not resort to complicated exercises and great care is taken to avoid strain. It is perfectly easy for me, a contralto, to sing C *in alt*

[*an Italianization of the (First) Norn in Wagner's *Götterdämmerung*] but do you suppose I sing it in my daily exercises? It is one of the extreme notes in my range and it might be a strain. Consequently I avoid it. I also sing most of my exercises *mezza voce*.

There should always be periods of intermission between practice. I often go about my routine work while on tour, walking up and down the room, packing my trunk, etc., and practicing gently at the same time. I enjoy it and it makes my work lighter.

Of course I take great pains to practice carefully. My exercises are for the most part simple scales, arpeggios or trills. For instance, I will start with the following:

This I sing in middle voice and very softly. Thereby I do not become tired and I don't bother the neighborhood. If I sang this in the big, full lower tones and sang loud, my voice would be fatigued rather than benefited and the neighbors would hate me. This I continue up to D or E flat.

Above this I invariably use what is termed the head tone. Female singers should always begin the head tone on this degree of the staff and not on F and F#, as is sometimes recommended.

I always use the Italian vowel "ah" in my exercises. It seems best to me. I know that "oo" and "ue" are recommended for contraltos, but I have long had the firm conviction that one should first perfect the natural vocal color through securing good tones by means of the most open vowel. After this is done the voice may be further colored by the judicious employment of other vowels. Sopranos, for instance, can help their head tones by singing "ee" (Italian *i*).

I know nothing better for acquiring a flexible tone than to sing trills like the following:

etc.

and at the same time preserve a gentle, smiling expression. Smile naturally, as though you were genuinely amused at something—smile until your upper teeth are uncovered. Then, try these exercises with the vowel "ah." Don't be afraid of getting a trivial, colorless tone. It is easy enough to make the tone sombre by willing it so, when the occasion demands. You will be amazed what this smiling, genial, *liebenswürdig** expression will do to relieve stiffness and help you in placing your voice right. The old Italians knew about it and advocated it strongly. There is nothing like it to keep the voice youthful, fresh and in the prime of condition.

The Singer Must Relax

Probably more voices are ruined by strain than through any other cause. The singer must relax all the time. This does not mean flabbiness. It does not mean that the singer should collapse before singing. Relaxation in the singer's sense is a delicious condition of buoyancy, of lightness, of freedom, of ease and entire lack of tightening in any part. When I relax I feel as though every atom in my body were floating in space. There is not one single little nerve or tension. The singer must be particularly careful when approaching a climax in a great work of art. Then the tendency to tighten up is at its greatest. This must be anticipated.

Take such a case as the following passage from the famous aria from Saint-Saëns' *Samson et Dalila,* "Mon coeur s'ouvre à ta voix." The climax is obviously on the words "Ah!—verse-moi." The climax is the note marked by a star (f on the top line).

When I am singing the last notes of the previous phrase to the word "tendresse," anyone who has observed me closely will notice that I instinctively let my shoulders drop—that the facial muscles become relaxed

[*amiable, charming]

as when one is about to smile or about to yawn. I am then relaxing to meet the great melodic climax and meet it in such a manner that I will have abundant reserve force after it has been sung. When one has to sing before an audience of five or six thousand people such a climax is immensely important and it requires great balance to meet it and triumph in it.

❧

Singing in Concert and What It Means

by
EMMA THURSBY

[Biographical sketch by James Francis Cooke]

[Emma Thursby was born in Brooklyn, N. Y., and studied singing with Julius Meyers, Achille Errani, Mme. Rudersdorf, Lamperti (elder), San Giovanni and finally with Maurice Strakosch. She began her career as a church singer in New York and throngs went to different New York churches to hear her exquisitely mellow and beautiful voice. For many years she was the soprano of the famous Plymouth Church when Henry Ward Beecher was the pastor. Her voice became so famous that she went on a tour with Maurice Strakosch for seven years, in Europe and America, everywhere meeting with sensational success. Later she toured with the Gilmore Band and with the Thomas Orchestra. She became as popular in London and in Paris as in New York. Her fame became so great that she finally made a tour of the world, appearing with great success even in China and Japan.]

Although conditions have changed very greatly since I was last regularly engaged in making concert tours, the change has been rather one of advantage to young singers than one to their disadvantage. The enormous advance in musical taste can only be expressed by the word "startling." For while we have apparently a vast amount of worthless music being continually inoculated into our unsuspecting public, we have, nevertheless, a corresponding cultivation of the love for good music which contributes much to the support of the concert singer of the present day.

The old-time lyceum has almost disappeared, but the high-class song recital has taken its place and recitals that would have been barely possible years ago are now frequently given with greatest financial and artistic success. Schumann, Franz, Strauss, Grieg and MacDowell have conquered the field formerly held by the vapid and meaningless compositions of brainless composers who wrote solely to amuse or to appeal to morbid sentimentality.

The conditions of travel, also, have been greatly improved. It is now possible to go about in railroad cars and stop at hotels, and at the same time experience very little inconvenience and discomfort. This makes the career of the concert artist a far more desirable one than in former years. Uninviting hotels, frigid cars, poorly prepared meals and the lack of privacy were scarcely the best things to stimulate a high degree of musical inspiration.

HEALTH

Nevertheless, the girl who would be successful in concert must either possess or acquire good health as her first and all-essential asset. Notwithstanding the marvelous improvement in traveling facilities and accommodations, the nervous strain of public performance is not lessened, and it not infrequently happens that these very facilities enable the avaricious manager to crowd in more concerts and recitals than in former years, with the consequent strain upon the vitality of the singer.

Of course, the singer must also possess the foundation for a good natural voice, a sense of hearing capable of being trained to the keenest perception of pitch, quality, rhythm and metre, an attractive personality, a bright mind, a good general education and an artistic temperament—a very extraordinary list, I grant you, but we must remember that the public pays out its money to hear extraordinary people and the would-be singer who does not possess qualifications of this description had better sincerely solicit the advice of some experienced, unbiased teacher or singer before putting forth upon the musical seas in a bark which must meet with certain destruction in weathering the first storm. The teacher who consciously advises a singer to undertake a public career and at the same time knows that such a career would very likely be a failure is beneath the recognition of any honest man or woman.

THE SINGER'S EARLY TRAINING

The education of the singer should not commence too early, if we mean by education the training of the voice. If you discover that a child has a very remarkable voice, "ear" and musical intelligence you had better let the voice alone and give your attention to the general musical education of the child along the lines of that received by Madame Sembrich, who is a fine violinist and pianist. So few are the teachers who know anything whatever about the child-voice, or who can treat it with any degree of safety, that it is far better to leave it alone than to tamper with it. Encourage the child to sing softly, sweetly and naturally, much as in free fluent conversation, telling him to form the habit of speaking his tones forward "on the lips" rather than in the throat. If you have among your acquaintances some musician or singer of indisputable ability and impeccable honor who can give you disinterested advice, have the child go to this friend now and then to ascertain whether any bad and unnatural habits are being formed. Of course we have the famous cases of Patti and others, who seem to have sung from infancy. I have no recollection of the time when I first commenced to sing. I have always sung and gloried in my singing.

See to it that your musical child has a good general education. This does not necessarily mean a college or university training. In fact, the amount of music study a singer has to accomplish in these days makes the higher academic training apparently impossible. However, with the great musical advance there has come a demand for higher and better ordered intellectual work among singers. This condition is becoming more and more imperative every day. At the same time you must remember also that nothing should be undertaken that might in any way be liable to undermine or impair the child's health.

When to Begin Training

The time to begin training depends upon the maturity of the voice and the individual, considered together with the physical condition of the pupil. Some girls are ready to start voice work at sixteen, while others are not really in condition until a somewhat older age. Here again comes the necessity for the teacher of judgment and experience. A teacher who might in any way be influenced by the necessity for securing a pupil or a fee should be avoided as one avoids the shyster lawyer. Starting vocal instruction too early has been the precipice over which many a promising career has been dashed to early oblivion.

In choosing a teacher I hardly know what to say, in these days of myriad methods and endless claims. The greatest teachers I have known have been men and women of great simplicity and directness. The perpetrator of the complicated system is normally the creator of vocal failures. The secret of singing is at once a marvelous mystery and again an open secret to those who have realized its simplicity. It cannot be altogether written, nor can it be imparted by words alone. Imitation undoubtedly plays an important part, but it is not everything. The teacher must be one who has actually realized the great truths which underlie the best, simplest and most natural methods of securing results and who must possess the wonderful power of exactly communicating these principles to the pupil. A good teacher is far rarer than a good singer. Singers are often poor teachers, as they destroy the individuality of the pupil by demanding arbitrary imitation. A teacher can only be judged by results, and the pupil should never permit herself to be deluded by advertisements and claims a teacher is unable to substantiate with successful pupils.

HABITS OF SPEECH, POISE AND THINKING

One of the deep foundation piers of all educational effort is the inculcation of habits. The most successful voice teacher is the one who is most happy in developing habits of correct singing. These habits must be watched with the persistence, perseverance and affectionate care of the scientist. The teacher must realize that the single lapse or violation of a habit may mean the ruin of weeks or months of hard work.

One of the most necessary habits a teacher should form is that of speaking with ease, naturalness and vocal charm. Many of our American girls speak with indescribable harshness, slovenliness and shrillness. This is a severe tax upon the sensibilities of a musical person and I know of countless people who suffer acute annoyance from this source. Vowels are emitted with a nasal twang or a throaty growl that seem at times most unpardonable noises when coming from a pretty face. Consonants are juggled and mangled until the words are very difficult to comprehend. Our girls are improving in this respect, but there is still cause for grievous complaint among voice teachers, who find in this one of their most formidable obstacles.

Another common natural fault, which is particularly offensive to me, is that of an objectionable bodily poise. I have found throughout my entire career that bodily poise in concert work is of paramount importance, but I seem to have great difficulty in sufficiently impressing this great truth upon young ladies who would be singers. The noted Parisian teacher Sbriglia is said to require one entire year to build up and fortify the chest. I have always felt that the best poise is that in which the shoulders are held well back, although not in a stiff or strained position, the upper part of the body leaning forward gently and naturally and the whole frame balanced by a sense of relaxation and ease. In this position the natural equilibrium is not taxed, and a peculiar sensation of non-constraint seems to be noticeable, particularly over the entire area of the front of the torso. This position suggests ease and an absence of that military rigidity which is so fatal to all good vocal effort. It also permits of a freer movement of the abdominal walls, as well as the intercostal muscles, and is thus conducive to the most natural breathing. Too much anatomical explanation is liable to confuse the young singer, and if the matter of breathing can be assisted by poise, just so much is gained.

Another important habit that the teacher should see to at the start is that of correct thinking. Most vocal beginners are poor thinkers and fail to realize the vast importance of the mind in all voice work. Unless the teacher has the power of inspiring the pupil to a realization of the great fact that nothing is accomplished in the throat that has not been previously performed in the mind, the path will be a difficult one. During the process of singing, the throat and the auxiliary vocal process of breathing are really a part of the brain, or, more specifically, the mind or soul. The body is never more than an instrument. Without the performer it is as voiceless as the piano of Richard Wagner standing in all its solitary silence at Wahnfried—a mute monument of the marvelous thoughts which once rang from its vibrating wires to all parts of the civilized world. We really sing with that which leaves the body after death. It is in the cultivation of this mystery of mysteries, the soul, that most singers fail. The mental ideal is, after all, that which makes the singer. Patti possessed this ideal as a child, and with it the wonderful bodily qualifications which made her immortal. But it requires work to overcome vocal deficiencies, and Patti as a child was known to have been a ceaseless worker and thinker, always trying to bring her little body up to the high æsthetic appreciation of the best artistic interpretation of a given passage.

MAURICE STRAKOSCH'S TEN VOCAL COMMANDMENTS

It was from Maurice Strakosch that I learned of the methods pursued by Patti in her daily work, and although Strakosch was not a teacher in the commercial sense of the word, as he had comparatively few pupils, he was nevertheless a very fine musician, and there is no doubt that Patti owed a great deal to his careful and insistent regime and instruction. Although our relation was that of impresario and artist, I cannot be grateful enough to him for the advice and instruction I received from him. The technical exercises he employed were exceedingly simple and he gave more attention to how they were sung than to the exercises themselves. I know of no more effective set of exercises than Strakosch's ten daily exercises. They were sung to the different vowels, principally to the vowel "ah," as in *father.* Notwithstanding their great simplicity Strakosch gave the greatest possible attention and time to them. Patti used these exercises, which he called his "Ten Commandments for the Singer," daily, and there can be little doubt that the extraordinary preservation of her voice is the result of these simple means. I have used them for years with exceptional results in all cases. However, if the singer has any idea that the mere practice of these exercises to the different vowel sounds will inevitably bring success she is greatly mistaken. These exercises are only valuable when used with vowels correctly and naturally "placed," and that means, in some cases, years of the most careful and painstaking work.

Following are the famous "Ten Vocal Commandments," as used by Adelina Patti and several great singers in their daily work. Note their simplicity and gradual increase in difficulty. They are to be transposed at the teacher's discretion to suit the range of the voice and are to be used with the different vowels.

V

VI

VII

VIII

IX

X

The concert singer of the present day must have linguistic attainments far greater than those in demand some years ago. She is required to sing in English, French, German, Italian and some singers are now attempting the interpretation of songs in Slavic and other tongues. Not only do we have to consider arias and passages from the great oratorios and operas as a part of the present-day repertoire, but the song of the "Lied" type has come to have a valuable significance in all concert work. Many songs intended for the chamber and the salon are now included in programs of concerts and recitals given in our largest auditoriums. Only a very few numbers are in themselves songs written for the concert hall. Most of the numbers now sung at song concerts are really transplanted from either the stage or the chamber. This makes the position of the concert singer an extremely difficult one. Without the dramatic accessories of the opera house or the intimacy of the home circle, she is expected to achieve results varying from the cry of the Valkyries, in *Die Walküre,* to the frail fragrance of Franz's "Es hat die Rose sich beklagt." I do not wonder that Mme. Schumann-Heink and others have declared that there is nothing more difficult or exhausting than concert singing. The enormous fees paid to great concert singers are not surprising when we consider how very few must be the people who can ever hope to attain great heights in this work.

❦

New Aspects of the Art of Singing in America

by

REINALD WERRENRATH

[Biographical sketch by James Francis Cooke]

[Reinald Werrenrath was born in Brooklyn, N. Y., August 7th, 1883. His father, George Werrenrath, was a distinguished singer, and his mother (née Aretta Camp) is the daughter of Henry Camp, who was for many years musical director of Plymouth Church during the ministry there of Henry Ward Beecher. George Werrenrath was a Dane, with an unusually rich tenor voice, trained by the best teachers of his time in Germany, Italy, France and England. During his engagement as leading tenor in the Royal Opera House in

Wiesbaden, he left Germany by the advice of Adelina Patti, eventually going to England with Maurice Strakosch, who was then his coach. In London Werrenrath had a fine career, and there was formed a warm and intimate friendship with Charles Gounod, with whom he studied and toured in concerts through England and Belgium. George Werrenrath came to New York in 1876, by the influence of Mme. Antoinette Sterling and of the well-known Dane, General C. T. Christensen. He immediately became well known by his appearance with the Theodore Thomas Orchestra, as well as by his engagement at Plymouth Church, where he was soloist for seven years. He was probably the first artist to give song-recitals in the United States, while his performances in opera are still cherished in the memories of those people who can look back on some of the fine representations given under the baton of Adolph Neuendorf, at the old Academy of Music, which made the way for the later work at the Metropolitan Opera House. His interpretation of *Lohengrin* was adjudged most wonderfully poetical.

Reinald Werrenrath studied first with his father. At the Boys' High School and at New York University he was leader of musical affairs throughout the eight years spent in those schools. He studied violin with Carl Venth for four years, and had as his vocal teachers Dr. Carl Dufft, Frank King Clark, Dr. Arthur Mees, Percy Rector Stephens and Victor Maurel, giving especial credit for his voice training to years of study with Mr. Stephens whose vocal teaching ideas he sketches in part in the following. He has appeared with immense success in concert and oratorio in all parts of the United States. His talking-machine records have been in great demand for years, and his voice is known to thousands who have never seen him. His operatic debut was in *Pagliacci*, as Silvio, in the Metropolitan Opera House, February 19th, 1919, where he later had specially fine success as Valentine in *Faust* and as the Toreador in *Carmen*.]

Every now and then someone asks me whether America is really becoming musical. All I can say is that a year ago I, with my accompanist, traveled over 61,000 miles, touching every part of this country and, during that eight months, singing almost nightly when the transit facilities would permit, found everywhere the very greatest enthusiasm for the very best music. Of course, Americans want some numbers on the program with the so-called "human" element; but at the same time they court the best in vocal art and seem never to get enough of it. All of my instruction has been received in America. All of my teachers, with the exception of my father and Victor Maurel, were born in America; so I may be called very much of an American product.

Just why Americans should ever have been obsessed with the idea that it was impossible to teach voice successfully on this side of the Atlantic is hard to tell. I have a suspicion that many like the adventure of foreign travel far more than the labor of study. Probably ninety-five per cent. of the pupils who went over did so for the fascinating experience of living in a European environment rather than for the downright purpose of coming back great artists. Therefore, we should not blame the European teachers altogether for the countless failures that have floated back to us almost on every tide. I have recently heard a report that many of the highest-priced and most efficient voice teachers in Italy are Americans who have Italianized their names. Certainly the most successful voice teachers in Berlin were George Ferguson and Frank King Clark, who was at the top of the list also in Paris when he was there.

The American singer should remember in these days that, first of all, he must sing in America and in the English language more than in any other. I am not one of those who decry singing in foreign languages. Certain songs, it is true, cannot be translated so that their meaning can be completely understood in English; yet, if the reader will think for a moment, how is the American auditor to understand a single thought of a poem in a language of which he knows nothing?

The Italian is a glorious language for the singer, and with it English cannot be compared, with its thirty-one vowel sounds and its many coughing, sputtering consonants. Training in Italian solfeggios is very fine for creating a free, flowing style. Many of the Italian teachers were obsessed with the idea of the big tone. The audiences fired back volleys of "Bravos!" and "Da Capos" when the tenor took off his plumed hat, stood on his toes and howled a high C. That was part of his stock in trade. Naturally, he forced his voice, and most of the men singers quit at the age of fifty. I hope to be in my prime at that time, as my voice seems to grow better each year. Battistini, who was born in 1857, is an exception. His voice, I am told, is remarkably preserved.

CLIMATIC CONDITIONS A SERIOUS HANDICAP

Climatic conditions in many parts of America prove a serious handicap to the singer. At the same time, according to the law of the survival of the fittest, American singers must take care of themselves much better than the Italians, for instance. The salubrious, balmy climate of most of Italy is ideal for the throat. On our Eastern seaboard I find that fifty per cent. of my audiences in winter seem to have colds and bronchitis. The singer who is obliged to tour must, of course, take every possible precaution against catching cold; and that means becoming infected from exposure to colds when the system is run down. I attempt to avoid colds by securing plenty of outdoor exercise. I always walk to my hotel and to the station when I have time; and I walk as much as I can during the day. When I am not singing

I immediately start to play—to fish, swim or hunt in the woods if I can make an opportunity.

OPERATIC STUDY

In one respect Europe is unquestionably superior to America for the vocal student. The student who wants to sing in opera will find in Europe ten opportunities for gaining experience to one here. While we have a few more opera companies than twenty-five years ago, it is still a great task to secure even an opening. Americans, outside of the great cities, do not seem to be especially inclined toward opera. They will accept a little of it when it is given to them by a superb company like the Metropolitan. In New York we find a public more cosmopolitan than in any other city of the world, with the possible exception of London. In immediate ancestry it is more European than American, and naturally opera becomes a great public demand. Seats sell at fabulous prices and the houses are crowded. Next comes opera at popular prices; and we have one or two very good companies giving that with success. Then there is the opera in America's other cosmopolitan center, Chicago, where many world-famed artists appear. After that, opera in America is hardly worth mentioning. What chance has the student? Only one who for years has been uniformed in a black dress suit and backed into the curve of the grand piano in a recital hall can know what it means to get out on the operatic stage, in those fantastic clothes, walk around, act, sing and at the same time watch the conductor with his ninety men. Only he can know what the difference between singing in concert and on the operatic stage really is. Yet old opera singers who enter the recital field invariably say that it is far harder to get up alone in a large hall and become the whole performance, aided and abetted only by an able accompanist, than it is to sing in opera.

The recital has the effect of preserving the fineness of many operatic voices. Modern opera has ruined dozens of fine vocal organs because of the tremendous strain made upon them and the tendency to neglect vocal art for dramatic impression.

If there were more of the better *singing* in opera, such as one hears from Mr. Caruso, there would be less comment upon opera as a bastard art. Operatic work is very exhilarating. The difference between concert and opera for the singer is that between oatmeal porridge and an old vintage champagne. There is no time at the Metropolitan for raw singers. The works in the repertoire must be known so well in the singing and the acting that they may be put on perfectly with the least possible rehearsals. Therefore, the singer has no time for routine. The lack of a foreign name will keep no American singer out of the Metropolitan; but the lack of the ability to save the company hundreds of dollars through needless waits at rehearsals will.

NATURAL METHODS OF SINGING

Certainly no country in recent years has produced so many "corking" good singers as America. Our voices are fresh, virile, pure and rich; when the teaching is right. Our singers are for the most part finely educated and know how to interpret the texts intelligently. Mr. W. J. Henderson, the eminent New York critic, in his *Art of Singing,* gave the following definition, which my former teacher, the late Dr. Carl Dufft, endorsed very highly: "Singing is the expression of a text by means of tones made by the human voice." More and more the truth of this comes to me. Singing is not merely vocalizing but always a means of communication in which the artist must convey the message of the two great minds of the poet and the composer to his fellow man. In this the voice must be as natural as possible, as human as possible, and not merely a sugary tone. The German, the Frenchman, the Englishman and the American strive first for an intelligent interpretation of the text. The Italian thinks of tone first and the text afterward, except in the modern Italian school of realistic singing. For this one must consider the voice normally and sensibly.

I owe my treatment of my voice largely to Mr. Stephens, with whom I have studied for the last eight years, taking a lesson every day I am in New York. This is advisable, I believe, because no matter how well one may think one sings, another trained mind with other ears may detect defects that might lead to serious difficulties later. His methods are difficult to describe; but a few main principles may be very interesting to vocalists.

My daily work in practice is commenced by stretching exercises, in which I aim to free the muscles covering the upper part of the abdomen and the intercostal muscles at the side and back—all by stretching upward and writhing around, as it were, so that there cannot possibly be any constriction. Then, with my elbows bent and my fists over my head, I stretch the muscles over my shoulders and shoulder blades. Finally, I rotate my head upward and around, so that the muscles of the neck are freed and become very easy and flexible. While I am finishing with the last exercise I begin speaking in a fairly moderate tone such vowel combinations as "oh-ah," "oh-ah," "ee-ay," "ee-ay," "ee-ay-ee-ay-ee-ay," etc. While doing this I walk about the room so that there will not be any suggestion of stiltedness or vocal or muscular interference. At first this is done without the addition of any attempted nasal resonance. Gradually nasal resonance is introduced with different spoken vowels, while at the same time every effort is made to preserve ease and flexibility of the entire body. Then, when it seems as though the right vocal quality is coming, pitch is introduced at the most convenient range and exercises with pitch are taken through the range of the voice. The whole idea is to make the tones as natural and free and pure as possible with the least effort. I am opposed to the old idea of tone placing, in which the pupil toed a mark, set the throat at some prescribed angle, adjusted the tongue in some approved design, and then, gripped like the unfortunate victim in the old-fashioned photographer's irons, attempted to sing a sustained tone or a rapid scale. What was the result—consciousness and stiltedness and, as a rule, a tired throat and a ruined singer. These ideas may seen revolutionary to many. They are only a few of Mr. Stephens' very numerous devices; but for many years they have been of more benefit than anything else in keeping me vocally fit.

We in the New World should be on the outlook for advance along all lines. Our American composers have held far too close to European ideals and done too little real thinking for themselves. Our vocal teachers and, for that matter, teachers in all branches of musical art in America have been most progressive in devising new ways and better methods. There will never be an American method of singing because we are too wise not to realize that every pupil needs different and special treatment. What is fine for one might be injurious to the next one.

❧

How I Regained a Lost Voice

by

HARRY EVAN WILLIAMS

[Biographical sketch by James Francis Cooke]

[Evan Williams, as his name suggests, was of Welsh ancestry, although born in Trumbull County, Ohio, Sept. 7th, 1867. As a boy his singing attracted the attention of his friends and neighbors. When a young man he went to Mme. Louise von Fielitsen, in Cleveland, and studied under her for four years. At the end of this time it became necessary for him to earn money immediately, as he had married at the age of twenty. Accordingly he went with the "Primrose and West" minstrels for one season. Everywhere he appeared his voice attracted enthusiastic attention. This aroused his ambition and in 1894 he went to New York where he was engaged at All Angels Church at a yearly salary of $1000. Six months later the Marble Collegiate Church took him over at $1500, which was shortly raised to $2000. In 1896 he appeared at the Worcester Festival with great success and then went to New York to study with James Sauvage for three years.

Notwithstanding his long terms of instruction with teachers of high reputation. Mr. Williams felt that he had still much to learn, as he would find himself singing finely one night and so badly on the next that he would resolve never to sing again. Accordingly he studied with Meehan for three years more. Then he retired from the concert stage for three years in order to improve himself. Deciding to appear in public again he went to London where he sang for three years with popular success. However, he was still dissatisfied with his voice. Mr. Williams' personal narrative tells how he got his voice back. His death, May 24th, 1918, prevented him from carrying out his project to become a teacher and thus introduce his discoveries. The following, therefore, becomes of interesting historical significance.]

There is nothing so disquieting to the singer as the feeling that his voice, upon which his artistic hopes, to say nothing of his livelihood, depend, is not a reliable organ, but a fickle thing which to-day may be in splendid condition but to-morrow may be gone. Time and again I have been driven to the verge of desperation by my own voice. While I am grateful to all of my excellent teachers for the many valuable things they taught me, I had a strong feeling that there was something which I must know and which only I myself could find out for myself. After a very wide experience here and in England I found myself with so little confidence in my ability to produce uniformly excellent results when on the concert stage, that I retired to Akron, Ohio, resolving to spend the rest of my life in teaching. There I remained for four years, thinking out the great problem that confronted me. It is only during the last year that I have become convinced that I have solved it. My musical work has made me well-to-do and I want now to give my ideas to the world so that others may profit if they find them valuable. I have nothing to sell—but I trust that I can put into words, without inventing a new and bewildering nomenclature, something that will prove of practical assistance to young singers as it has been to me.

AN INDISPUTABLE RECORD

In 1908 I left Akron and resolved to try to reinstate myself in New York as a singer. I also made talking-machine records, only to find that seldom could I make a record at the first attempt that was up to the very high standard maintained by the company in the case of all records placed upon the market for sale. This meant a great waste of my time and the company's material and services. It naturally set me thinking. If I could do it one time—

why couldn't I do it all the time? There was no contradicting the talking-machine record. The machine records the slightest blemish as well as the most perfect tone. There was no getting away from the fact that sometimes my singing was far from what I wished it to be.

The strange thing about it all was that my singing did not seem to depend upon the physical condition or feeling of my throat. Some days when my throat felt at its very best the records would come back in a way that I was ashamed of. It is a strange feeling to hear one's own voice from the talking machine. It sounds quite differently from the impression one gets while singing. I began to ponder, why were some of my records poor and others good?

After deep thought for a very long period of time, I commenced to make certain postulates which I believe I have since proved (to my own satisfaction at least) to be reasonable and true. They not only resulted in an improvement in my voice, but they enabled me to do at command what I had previously been able to do only occasionally. They are:

I. Tone creates its own support.
II. Much of the time spent in elaborate breathing exercises (while excellent for the health and valuable to the singer, in a way) do not produce the results that are expected.
III. The singer's first studies should be with his brain and ear, rather than through an attempt at muscular control of the breathing muscles.
IV. Vocal resonance can be developed through a proper understanding of tone color (vocal timbre), so that uniformly excellent production of tones will result.

Tone Creates Its Own Support

The first two postulates can be discussed as one. Tone creates its own support. How does a bird learn to sing? How does the animal learn to cry? How does the lion learn to roar? Or the donkey learn to bray? By practicing breathing exercises? Most certainly not. I have known many, many singers with splendid voices who have never heard of breathing exercises. Go out into the Welsh mining districts and listen to the voices. They learn to breathe by learning how to sing, and by singing. These men have lungs that the average vocal student would give a fortune to possess. By singing correctly they acquire all the lung control that any vocal composition could demand.

As a matter of fact, one does not need such a huge amount of breath to sing. The average singer uses entirely too much. A goose has lungs ten times as large as a nightingale but that doesn't make the goose's song lovely to listen to. I have known men with lungs big enough to work a blast furnace who yet had little bits of voices, so small that they were ridiculous. It would be better for most vocal students to emit the breath for five seconds before attacking the tone. One of the reasons for much vocal forcing is too much breath. Maybe I haven't thought about these things! I have spent hours in silence making up my mind. It is my firm conviction that the average person (entirely without instruction in breathing of a special kind) has enough breath to sing any phrase one might be called upon to sing. I think, without question, that teachers and singers have all been working their heads off to develop strength in the wrong direction. Mind you—this is not a sermon against breathing. I believe in plenty of breathing exercises for the sake of one's health.

A GOOD POSITION

Singers study breathing as though they were trying to learn how to push out the voice or pull it out by suction. By standing in a sensible position with the chest high (but not forced up), the lung capacity of the average individual is quite surprising. A good position can be secured through the old Delsarte exercise which is as follows:

I. Stand on the balls of your feet, heels just touching the floor.
II. Hold your arms at your side in a relaxed condition.
III. Move your arms forward until they form an angle of forty-five degrees with the body. Press the palms down until the chest is up comfortably.
IV. Now let your arms drop back without letting your chest fall. Feel a sense of ease and freedom over the whole body. Breathe naturally and deeply.

In other words, to "poise" the breath, stand erect, at attention. Most people when called to this "attention" posture stiffen themselves so that they are in a position of resistance. When I say *attention*—I mean the position in which you have alertness but at the same time complete freedom—when you can freely smile, sigh, scowl and sneer—the attention that will permit expansion of the chest with every change of mood. Then, open the mouth without inhaling. Let the breath out for five seconds, close the mouth and inhale through the nostrils. I keep the fact that I breathe into the lungs through the nostrils before me all the time. Again open the mouth without allowing the air to pass in. Practice this until a comfortable stretch is felt in the flesh of the face, the top of the head, the back, the chest and the abdomen. If you stretch violently you will not experience this feeling.

SENSATIONS

I fully realize that much of what I have said will not be in accord with what is preached, practiced and taught by many vocal teachers and I cannot attempt to reply to any critics. I merely know what sensations and experiences I have had after a lifetime of practical work in a profession which has brought me a fortune. Furthermore I know that anything anyone might say on the subject of the human voice would be at variance with the opinions of others. There is probably no subject in human ken in which there is such a marked difference of opinion. I can merely try to describe my own sensations and vocal experiences. In trying to represent the course of the sensation I experience in producing a good tone, I have employed the following illustration. Imagine two pieces of whip cord. Tie the ends together. Place the knot immediately under the upper lip directly beneath the center bone of the nose, run the strings straight back for an inch, then up over the cheek bones, then down around the uvula, thence down the large cords inside the neck. At a point in the center between the shoulders the cords would split in order to let one set go down the back and the other toward the chest, meeting again under the arm-pits, thence down the short ribs, thence down and joining in another knot slightly back of the pelvic bone. Laugh, if you will, but this is actually the sensation I have repeatedly felt in producing what the talking machine has shown to be a good tone. Remember that there were plenty to laugh at Columbus, Galileo and even Darius Green of the Flying Machine.

Stand in "attention" as directed, with the body responsive and the mind sensitive to physical impressions. When opening the mouth without taking in air, a slight stretch will be experienced along the whole track I have described. The poise felt in this position is what permitted Bob Fitzsimmons to strike a deadly blow with a two-inch stroke. It is the responsive poise with which I sing both loud and soft tones. Furthermore, I do not believe in an absolutely relaxed lower jaw as though it had been broken. Who could sing with a broken jaw?—and a broken jaw would represent ideal relaxation. The jaw should be slightly stretched but never strained. I think that the word "relaxation," as used by most teachers and as understood by most students, is responsible for more ruined voices than all other terms used in vocal teaching. I have talked this matter over with numberless great singers who are constantly before the public, and their very singing is the best contradiction of this. When you hold your hand out freely before you what is it that keeps it from falling at your side? That same condition controls the jaw. Find it: it is not relaxation. If you would be a perfect singer find the juggler who is balancing a feather. Imagine yourself poised on the top of that feather, and sing without falling off.

Contrasting Timbres
that Lead to a Beautiful Tone When Combined

We shall now seek to illustrate two contrasting qualities of tones, between which lies that quality which I sought for so long. The desired quality is not a compromise, but seems to be located half way between two extremes, and may best be brought to the attention of the reader by describing the extremes.

The first is a dark quality of tone. To get this, place the tips of the second fingers on the sides of the voice box (Adam's apple) and make a dark almost breathy sound, using "u" as in the word *hum.* Do this without any signs of strain. Allow the sound to float up into the mouth and nose. To many there will also be a sensation as though the sound were also floating down into the lungs (into both lungs). Do not make any conscious effort to force the sound or place it in any particular location. The sound will do it of its own accord if you do not strain. While the sound is being made, there will be a slight upward pulling of the voice box, a slight tugging at the voice box. This, of course, occurs automatically, and there should be no attempt to control it or promote it. It is nature at work. The tongue, while making this sound, should be limp, with the tip resting on the lower front teeth. All along it is necessary to caution the singer not to strive to do artificial things. Therefore do not poke or stick the tip of your tongue against the front teeth. If your tongue is not strained it will rest there naturally. Work at this exercise until you can fill the mouth and nose (and also seemingly the chest) with a rich, smooth, well-controlled, well-modulated dark sound and do it easily—with slight effort. Do not try to hold the sound in the throat.

The second sound we shall experiment with is the extreme antithesis of the first sound. Its resonance is high and it is bright in every sense. Place the fingers on the joints just in front and above holes in the ears. Open the mouth without inhaling and make the sound of "e" as in *when.* As the dark sound described before cannot be made too dark, this sound cannot be made too strident. It is the extreme from the rumble of the drum to the piercing rasp of the file. I have called it the animal sound, and in calling it strident, please do not infer that the nose, or any part of the mouth or soft palate, should be pinched to make it nasal, in the restricted sense of that term. When I sing this tone it is accompanied with a sensation as though the tone were being reflected downward from the voice box over to each side of the chest just in front of the arm-pits and then downward into the abdomen. Here the great danger arises that the unskilled student will try to produce this sensation, whereas the fact of the matter is that the sensation is the accompaniment of the properly produced tone and cannot be made artificially. Don't work for the sensation, work for the tone that produces such a sensation. At the same time the tone has a sensation of upward reflection, as though it arose at the back of the voice box and separated there, passed up behind the jaws to the points where your fingers are resting, entering the mouth from above, as it were from a point just between the hard and soft palates, and becoming one sound in the mouth.

The uvula and part of the soft palate should be associated with the dark sound. The hard palate and part of the soft palate should be associated with the strident tone.

THE TONGUE POSITION

In making the strident sound the tongue should rest in the same position as for the dark sound. The dark tone never changes and is the basic sound which gives fullness, foundation, depth to the ultimate tone. Without it all voices are thin and unsubstantial. The nearer the singer gets to this the nearer he approaches the great vibrating base upon which the world is founded.

Remember that the dark tone never changes. It is the background, the canvas upon which the singer paints his infinite moods by means of different vowels, emotions, and the tone colors which are derived in numberless modifications from the strident tone. Another simile may bring the subject nearer to the reader student. Imagine the dark tone and all the sensations in different parts of the body as a kind of atmosphere or gas which requires to be set on fire by the electric spark of the strident tone. The dark tone is all necessary, but it is useless unless it is properly electrified by the strident tone.

A PRACTICAL STEP

How shall we utilize what we have learned, so that the student may convince himself that herein lies the truth which, properly understood and sensibly applied, will lead to a means of improving his tone. If the foregoing has been carefully read and understood, the following exercise to get the tone which results from a combination of the dark and the strident is simple.

I. Stand erect as directed.
II. Open the mouth *without inhaling.*
III. Produce the dark tone ("u" as in *hum*).
IV. Close the mouth and allow the air to pass in and out of the nostrils for a few seconds.
V. Open the mouth without inhaling.
VI. Make the strident sound ("e" as in *when*).

VII. Close the mouth and let the air pass in and out of nostrils a few seconds.

VIII. Open the mouth without inhaling.

IX. Sing the vowel "ah" as in *father* in such a manner that it is a combination of the dark tone and the strident tone.

X. Do this in such a way that all of the breathy disagreeable features of the dark tone disappear but its foundation features remain to give it fullness and roundness, while all of the disagreeable features of the strident tone disappear although its color-giving, light-giving, life-giving characteristics are retained to give the combination-tone richness and sweetness. A beautiful result is inevitable, if the principle is properly understood. I have tried this with many people who have sung but little before in their lives and who were not conscious of having interesting voices. Without a long course of vocal lessons or anything of the sort they have been able to produce in a short time— a very few minutes—a tone that would be admired by any critic.

A COMFORTABLE PITCH

It is to be assumed that the student will, in these experiments, take the pitch in his voice which is most comfortable. Having mastered the combination tone on "ah" at any pitch, it will be easy to try other pitches and other vowels. "Ah" is the natural vowel, but having secured the "know how" through a correct production of "ah," the same results may be attained with any other vowel produced in a similar way. "e" as in *see* has of course more of the strident quality, the high, bright quality and "oo" as in *moon* more of the dark, but even these extreme tones may be so placed that they become enriched through the employment of resonance of all those parts of the mouth, nose and body which may be brought naturally to reinforce them.

"PING"

I have never met a singer who was not looking for "ping" or what is called brightness. Most voices are hopelessly dead, and therefore lack sweetness. The voices are filled with night—black hollow gloomy night or else they are as strident as the caterwauling of a tomcat. The happy mean between the extremes is the area in which the singer's greatest results are attained.

Think of your tone, always. The breath will then take care of itself. If the tone has a tremolo, or sounds stuffy or sounds weak, you have not apportioned the right amount of breath to it, but you are not going to gain this information by thinking of the breath but by thinking of the tone.

LET YOUR OWN EARS CONVINCE YOU

Now, that is all there is to it. I am not striving to found a method or anything of the sort; but I have seen students waste years on what is called "voice placing" and not come to anything like the same result that will come after the accomplishment of this simple matter. Try it out with your own voice. You will see in a short time what it will do. Your own ears will convince you, to say nothing of the ears of your friends. All I know is that after I discovered this, it was possible for me to employ it and make records with so small a percentage of discard that I have been surprised.

It remains for the intelligent teachers to apply such knowledge to a systematic vocal course of exercises, studies and songs, which will help the pupil to progress most rapidly. Don't think that I am pretending to tell all that there is to vocal culture in an hour. It is a great and important study upon which I have spent a lifetime. However, as I said before, I have nothing to sell and I am only too happy to give this information which has cost me so many hours of thought to crystallize.

ॐ

Memory, Imagination, Analysis

An interview with
HERBERT WITHERSPOON

by Harriette Brower

No doubt the serious teacher, who may be occupied in any branch of musical activity, has often pictured to himself what an ideal institution of musical art might be like if all students assembled should study thoroughly their particular instrument, together with all that pertained to it. They should by all means possess talent, intelligence, industry, and be far removed from a superficial attitude toward their chosen field. The studio used for instruction in this imagined institution should also be ideal, quiet, airy, homelike, artistic.

Some such vision perhaps floats before the minds of some of us teachers when we are in the mood to dream of ideal conditions under which we would like to see our art work conducted.

It has been possible for Mr. Herbert Witherspoon, the distinguished basso and teacher, to make such a dream-picture come true. For he has established an institution of vocal art—in effect if not in name—where all the subjects connected with singing are considered and taught in the order of their significance. Not less ideal is the building which contains these studios, for Mr. Witherspoon has fitted up his private home as a true abiding place for the muse.

At the close of a busy day, marked like all the rest with a full complement of lessons, the master teacher was willing to relax a little and speak of the work in which he is so deeply absorbed. He apologized for having run over the time of the last lesson, saying he never could teach by the clock.

"I do not like to call this a school," he began, "although it amounts to one in reality, but only in so far as we take up the various subjects connected with vocal study. I consider languages of the highest importance; we have them taught here. There are classes in analysis, in pedagogy—teaching teachers how to instruct others. We have an excellent master for acting and for stage deportment: I advise that students know something of acting, even if they do not expect to go in for opera; they learn how to carry themselves and are more graceful and self-possessed before an audience.

"The work has developed far beyond my expectations. There are over two hundred students, and I have eight assistants who have been trained by me and know my ways and methods. Some of these give practice lessons to students, who alternate them with the lessons given by me. These lessons are quite reasonable, and in combination with my work, give the student daily attention.

"My plan is not to accept every applicant who comes, but to select the most promising. The applicants must measure up to a certain standard before they can enter. To this one fact is due much of our success."

"And what are these requirements?"

"Voice, to begin with; youth (unless the idea is to teach), good looks, musical intelligence, application. If the candidate possesses these requisites, we begin to work. In three months' time it can be seen whether the student is making sufficient progress to come up to our standard. Those who do not are weeded out. You can readily see that as a result of this weeding process, we have some very good material and fine voices to work with.

"We have many musicals and recitals, both public and private, where young singers have an opportunity to try their wings. There is a most generous, unselfish spirit among the students; they rejoice in each others' success, with never a hint of jealousy. We have had a number of recitals in both Æolian and Carnegie Halls, given by the artist students this season. On these occasions the other students always attend and take as much interest as though they were giving the recital themselves.

BEL CANTO

"You have remarked lately that 'singers are realizing that the lost art of *bel canto* is the thing to strive for and they are now searching for it.' Can you give a little more light on this point?"

"I hardly meant to say that in any sense the art of *bel canto* was lost; how could it be? Many singers seem to attach some uncanny significance to the term. *Bel canto* means simply *beautiful singing*. When you have perfect breath control, and distinct, artistic enunciation, you will possess *bel canto,* because you will produce your tones and your words beautifully.

"Because these magic words are in the Italian tongue does not mean that they apply to something only possessed by Italians. Not at all. Any one can sing beautifully who does so with ease and naturalness, the American just as well as those of any other countries. In fact I consider American voices, in general, better trained than those of Italy, Germany or France. The Italian, in particular, has very little knowledge of the scientific side; he usually sings by intuition.

"We ought to have our own standards in judging American voices; until we do so, we will be constantly comparing them with the voices of foreign singers. The quality of the American voice is different from the quality found in the voices of other countries. To my mind the best women's voices are found right here in our midst.

MEMORY

"I have also said that there are three great factors which should form the foundation stones upon which the singer should rear his structure of musical achievement. These factors are memory, imagination, analysis. I have put memory first because it is the whole thing, so to say. The singer without memory—a cultivated memory—does not get far. Memory lies at the very foundation of his work, and must continue with it the whole journey through, from the bottom to the top. In the beginning you think a beautiful tone, you try to reproduce it. When you come to it again you must remember just how you did it before. Each time you repeat the tone this effort of memory comes in, until at last it has become second nature to remember and produce the result; you now begin to do so automatically.

"As you advance there are words to remember as well as notes and tones. Memory, of course, is just as necessary for the pianist. He must be able to commit large numbers of notes, phrases and passages. In his case there are a number of keys to grasp at once, but the singer can sing but one tone at a time. Both notes and words should be memorized, so the singer can come before the audience without being confined to the printed page. When acting is added there is still more to remember. Back of memory study lies concentration; without concentration little can be accomplished in any branch of art.

IMAGINATION

"The central factor is imagination; what can be done without it! Can you think of a musician, especially a singer, without imagination? He may acquire the letter—that is, execute the notes correctly, but the performance is dead, without life or soul. With imagination he comprehends what is the inner meaning of the text, the scene; also what the composer had in mind when he wrote. Then he learns to express these emotions in his own voice and action, through the imaginative power, which will color his tones, influence his action, render his portrayal instinct with life. Imagination in some form is generally inherent in all of us. If it lies dormant, it can be cultivated and brought to bear upon the singer's work. This is absolutely essential.

ANALYSIS

"I have put analysis last because it is the crowning virtue, the prime necessity. We study analysis here in the studios, learning how to separate music into its component parts, together with simple chord formations, general form and structure of the pieces, and so on. Can you comprehend the dense ignorance of many music students on these subjects? They will come here to me, never having analyzed a bit of music in their lives, having not an inkling of what chord structure and form in music mean. If they played piano even a little, they could hardly escape getting a small notion of chord formation. But frequently vocal students know nothing of the piano. They are too apt to be superficial. It is an age of superficiality—and cramming: we see these evils all the way from the college man down. I am a Yale man and don't like to say anything about college government, yet I cannot shut my eyes to the fact that men may spend four years going through college and yet not be educated when they come out. Most of us are in too much of a hurry, and so fail to take time enough to learn things thoroughly; above all we never stop to analyze.

"Analysis should begin at the very outset of our vocal or instrumental study. We analyze the notes of the music we are singing, and a little later its form. We analyze the ideas of the composer and also our own thoughts and ideas, to try and bring them in harmony with his. After analyzing the passage before us, we may see it in a totally different light, and so phrase and deliver it with an entirely different idea from what we might have done without this intelligent study."

Conscious or Unconscious Control

"Do you advise conscious action of the parts comprising the vocal instrument, or do you prefer unconscious control of the instrument, with thought directed to the ideal quality in tone production and delivery?" was asked.

"By all means unconscious control," was the emphatic answer. "We wish to produce beautiful sounds; if the throat is open, the breathing correct, and we have a mental concept of that beautiful sound, we are bound to produce it. It might be almost impossible to produce correct tones if we thought constantly about every muscle in action. There is a great deal of nonsense talked and written about the diaphragm, vocal cords and other parts of the anatomy. It is all right for the teacher who wishes to be thoroughly trained to know everything there is to know about the various organs and muscles; I would not discourage this. But for the young singer I consider it unnecessary. Think supremely of the beautiful tones you desire to produce; listen for them with the outer ear—and the inner ear—that is to say—mentally—and you will hear them. Meanwhile, control is becoming more and more habitual, until it approaches perfection and at last becomes automatic. When that point is reached, your sound-producing instrument does the deed, while your whole attention is fixed on the interpretation of a master work, the performance of which requires your undivided application. If there is action, you control that in the same way until it also becomes automatic; then both singing and acting are spontaneous."

Does the Singer Hear Himself?

This question was put to Mr. Witherspoon, who answered:

"The singer of course hears himself, and with study learns to hear himself better. In fact I believe the lack of this part of vocal training is one of the greatest faults of the day, and that the singer should depend more upon hearing the sound he makes than upon feeling the sound. In other words, train the *ear,* the court of ultimate resort, and the only judge—and forget sensation as much as possible, for the latter leads to a million confusions.

"Undoubtedly a singer hears in his own voice what his auditors do not hear, for he also hears with his inner ear, but the singer must learn to hear his own voice as others hear it, which he can do perfectly well. Here we come to analysis again.

"The phonograph records teach us much in this respect, although I never have considered that the phonograph reproduces the human voice. It comes near it in some cases, utterly fails in others, and the best singers do not always make the best or most faithful reproductions."

The Coda

Concluding remarks by
HARRIETTE BROWER

A RESUMÉ

The student, seeking light on the many problems of vocal technic, the training for concert and opera, how to get started in the profession, and kindred subjects of vital importance, has doubtless found in the foregoing talks a rich fund of help and suggestion. It is from such high sources that a few words of personal experience and advice have often proved to be to the young singer a beacon light, showing what to avoid and what to follow. It were well to gather up these strands of suggestion from great artists and weave them into a strong bulwark of precept and example, so that the student may be kept within the narrow path of sound doctrine and high endeavor.

At the very outset, two points must be borne in mind:

1. Each and every voice and mentality is individual.
2. The artist has become a law unto himself; it is not possible for him to make rules for others.

First, as to difference in voices. When it is considered that the human instrument, unlike any fabricated by the hand of man, is a purely personal instrument, subject to endless variation through variety in formation of mouth and throat cavities, also physical conditions of the anatomy, it is no cause for wonder that the human instrument should differ in each individual. Then think of all sorts and conditions of mentality, environment, ambitions and ideals. It is a self-evident fact that the vocal instrument must be a part of each person, of whom there are "no two alike."

Artists in general have strongly expressed themselves on this point: most of them agree with Amelita Galli-Curci, when she says, "There are as many kinds of voices as there are persons; therefore it seems to me each voice should be treated in the manner best suited to its possessor." "Singing is such an individual thing, after all," says Anna Case, "it is a part of one's very self." "Each person has a different mentality and a different kind of voice," says Giovanni Martinelli; "indeed there are as many qualities of voice as there are people."

Granting, then, that there are no two voices and personalities in the world exactly alike, it follows, as a natural conclusion, that the renowned vocalist, who has won his or her way from the beginning up to fame and fortune, realizes that her instrument and her manner of training and handling it are peculiarly personal. As she has won success through certain means and methods, she considers those means belong to her, in the sense that they especially suit her particular instrument. She is then a law unto herself and is unwilling to lay down any laws for others. Geraldine Farrar does not imply there is only one right way to train the voice, and she has found that way. In speaking of her method of study, she says, "These things seem best for my voice, and this is the way I work. But, since each voice is different, my ways might not suit any one else. I have no desire to lay down rules for others; I can only speak of my own experience."

Galli-Curci says, "The singer who understands her business must know just how she produces tones and vocal effects. She can then do them at all times, even under adverse circumstances, when nervous or not in the mood. I have developed the voice and trained it in the way that seemed to me best for it. How can any other person tell you how that is to be done?"

"It rests with the singer what she will do with her voice—how she will develop it," remarks Louise Homer. Martinelli says, "The voice is a hidden instrument and eventually its fate must rest with its possessor. After general principles are understood, a singer must work them out according to his ability." Florence Easton remarks, "Each singer who has risen, who has found herself, knows by what path she climbed, but the path she found might not do for another."

Instead of considering this reticence on the part of the successful singer to explain the ways and means which enabled him to reach success, in the light of a selfish withholding of advice which would benefit the young student, we rather look upon it as a worthy and conscientious desire not to lead any one into paths which might not be best for his or her instrument.

In the beginning the student needs advice from an expert master, and is greatly benefited by knowing how the great singers have achieved. Later on, when principles have become thoroughly understood, the young singers learn what is best for their own voices; they, too, become a law unto themselves, capable of continuing the development of their own voices in the manner best suited to this most individual of all instruments.

AMERICAN VOICES

We often hear slighting things said of the quality of American voices, especially the speaking voice. They are frequently compared to the beauty of European voices, to the disparagement of those of our own country. Remembering the obloquy cast upon the American voice, it is a pleasure to record the views of some of the great singers on this point. "There are quantities of girls in America with good voices, good looks and a love for music," asserts Mme. Easton. Frieda Hempel says, "I find there are quantities of lovely voices here in America. The quality of the American female voice is beautiful; in no country is it finer, not even in Italy." Herbert Witherspoon, who has such wonderful experience in training voices, states, "We ought to have our own standards in judging American voices; until we do so we will be constantly comparing them with the voices of foreign singers. The quality of the American voice is different from the quality found in the voices of other countries. To my mind, the best women's voices are found right here in our midst." And he adds, "Any one can sing beautifully who does so with ease and naturalness, the American just as well as those of any other country. In fact I consider American voices, in general, better trained than those of Italy, Germany or France. The Italian, in particular, has very little knowledge of the scientific side; he usually sings by intuition."

AMERICAN VOICE TEACHERS

If this be accepted, that American voices are better trained than those of other countries, and there is no reason to doubt the statement of masters of such standing, it follows there must be competent instructors in the art of song right in our own land. Mme. Easton agrees with this. "There are plenty of good vocal teachers in America," she says, "not only in New York City, but in other large cities of this great country. There is always the problem, however, of securing just the right kind of a teacher. For a teacher may be excellent for one voice but not for another." Morgan Kingston asserts, "There is no need for an American to go out of his own country for vocal instruction or languages; all can be learned right here at home. I am a living proof of this. What I have done others can do." "You have excellent vocal teachers right here in America," says Mme. Hempel. Then she marvels, that with all these advantages at her door, there are not more American girls who make good. She lays it to the fact that our girls try to combine a social life with their musical studies, to the great detriment of the latter.

ARE AMERICAN VOCAL STUDENTS SUPERFICIAL?

It is doubtless a great temptation to the American girl who possesses a voice and good looks, who is a favorite socially, to neglect her studies at times for social gaiety. She is in such haste to make something of herself, to get where she can earn a little with her voice; yet by yielding to other calls she defeats the very purpose for which she is striving by a lowered ideal of her art. Let us see how the artists and teachers view this state of things.

Lilli Lehmann says: "The trouble with American girls is they are always in a hurry. They are not content to sit down quietly and study till they have developed themselves into something before they ever think of coming to Europe. They think if they can only come over here and sing for an artist, that fact alone will give them prestige in America. With us, American girls are too often looked upon as superficial because they come over here quite unprepared. I say to them: Go home and study; there are plenty of good teachers of voice and piano in your own land. Then, when you can *sing,* come here if you wish."

Frieda Hempel speaks from close observation when she says, "Here in America, girls do not realize the amount of labor and sacrifice involved, or they might not be so eager to enter upon a musical career. They are too much taken up with teas, parties, and social functions to have sufficient time to devote to vocal study and to all that goes with it. In order to study all the subjects required, the girl with a voice must be willing to give most of her day to work. This means sacrificing the social side, and being willing to throw herself heart and soul into the business of adequately preparing herself for her career."

The Vocal Student Must Not Be Afraid to Work

In the words of Caruso's message to vocal students, they must be willing "to work—to work always—and to sacrifice." But Geraldine Farrar does not consider this in the light of sacrifice. Her message to the young singer is: "Stick to your work and study systematically, whole-heartedly. If you do not love your work enough to give it your best thought, to make sacrifices for it, then there is something wrong with you. Better choose some other line of work, to which you can give undivided attention and devotion. For music requires both. As for sacrifices, they really do not exist if they promote the thing you honestly love most. You must never stop studying, for there is always so much to learn."

"I have developed my voice through arduous toil," to quote Mme. Galli-Curci. Rosa Raisa says, "One cannot expect to succeed in the profession of music without giving one's best time and thought to the work of vocal training and all the other subjects that go with it. A man in business gives his day, or the most of it, to his office. My time is devoted to my art, and indeed I have not any too much time to study all the necessary sides of it."

"I am always studying, always striving to improve what I have already learned and trying to acquire the things I find difficult, or have not yet attained to," testifies Mme. Homer.

THE REQUIREMENTS FOR A VOCAL CAREER

Those who have been through the necessary drudgery and struggle and have won out should be able to given an authoritative answer to this all-important question. They know what they started with, what any singer must possess at the beginning, and what she must acquire.

Naturally the singer must have a voice, for there is no use trying to cultivate something which does not exist. All artists subscribe to this. They also affirm she should have good looks, a love for music and a musical nature.

Let us hear from Mme. Homer on this subject: "1. Voice, first of all. 2. Intelligence; for intelligence controls, directs, shines through and illumines everything. What can be done without it? 3. Musical nature. 4. Capacity for work. Without application, the gifts of voice, intelligence and a musical nature will not make an artist. 5. A cheerful optimism, which refuses to yield to discouragement. 6. Patience. It is only with patient striving, doing the daily vocal task, and trying to do it each day a little better than the day before, that anything worth while is accomplished. The student must have unlimited patience to labor and wait for results."

Mr. Witherspoon states that students coming to him must possess "voice, to begin with; youth, good looks, musical intelligence and application. If the candidate possesses these requisites, we begin to work." Anna Case answers the question as to the vital requisites necessary to become a singer: "Brains, personality, voice."

Quotations could be multiplied to prove that all artists fully concur with those already mentioned. There must be a promising voice to cultivate, youth, good looks (for a public career) and the utmost devotion to work.

WHAT BRANCHES OF STUDY MUST BE TAKEN UP?

All agree there are many other subjects to study besides singing; that alone is far from sufficient. Edward Johnson says, "Singing itself is only a part, perhaps the smaller part of one's equipment. If opera be the goal, there are languages, acting, make up, impersonation, interpretation, how to walk, all to be added to piano, harmony and languages. The most important of all is a musical education."

Most of the great singers have emphatically expressed themselves in favor of piano study. Indeed, many were pianists in the beginning, before they began to develop the voice. Among those who had this training are: Galli-Curci, Lehmann, Raisa, Case, and Marguerite d'Alvarez, María Barrientos and Sophie Braslau. Miss Braslau says, "I am so grateful for my knowledge of the piano and its literature; it is the greatest help to me now.

To my thinking all children should have piano lessons; the cost is trifling compared with the benefits they receive. They should be made to study, whether they wish it or not, for they do not know what is best for them."

Mme. Raisa says, "There are so many sides to the singer's equipment besides singing itself. The piano is a necessity; the singer is greatly handicapped without a knowledge of that instrument, for it not only provides accompaniment but cultivates musical sense." "The vocal student should study piano as well as languages," asserts Mme. Homer; "both are the essentials. Not that she need strive to become a pianist; that would not be possible if she is destined to be a singer. But the more she knows of the piano and its literature, the more this will cultivate her musical sense and develop her taste."

Florence Easton is even more emphatic. "If a girl is fond of music, let her first study the piano, for a knowledge of the piano and its music is at the bottom of everything. All children should have this opportunity, whether they desire it or not. The child who early begins to study piano will often unconsciously follow the melody with her voice. Thus the love of song is awakened in her, and a little later it is discovered she has a voice worth cultivating."

On the subject of languages, artists are equally specific. Languages are an absolute necessity, beginning with one's mother tongue. The student should not imagine that, because he is born to the English language, it does not require careful study. Galli-Curci remarks, "The singer can always be considered fortunate who has been brought up to more than one language. I learned Spanish and Italian at home. In school I learned French, German and English, not only a little smattering of each, but how to write and speak them."

Rosa Raisa speaks eight languages, according to her personal statement: Russian, of course, as she is Russian, then French, Italian, German, Spanish, Polish, Roumanian and English.

"The duty is laid upon Americans to study other languages, if they expect to sing," says Florence Easton. "I know how often this study is neglected by the student. It is only another phase of that haste which is characteristic of the young student and singer."

BREATH CONTROL

Following the subject of requirements for a vocal career, let us get right down to the technical side, and review the ideas of artists on breath control, how to practice, what are the necessary exercises, what vowels should be used, and so on.

All admit that the subject of breath control is perhaps the most important of all. Lehmann says, "I practice many breathing exercises without using tone. Breath becomes voice through effort of will and by use of vocal organs. When singing, emit the smallest quantity of breath. Vocal cords are breath regulators; relieve them of all overwork."

Mme. Galli-Curci remarks, "Perhaps, in vocal mastery, the greatest factor of all is the breathing. To control the breath is what each student is striving to learn, what every singer endeavors to perfect, what every artist should master. It is an almost endless study and an individual one, because each organism and mentality is different."

Marguerite d'Alvarez: "In handling and training the voice, breathing is perhaps the most vital thing to be considered. To some breath control seems second nature; others must toil for it. With me it is intuition. Breathing is such an individual thing. With each person it is different, for no two people breathe in just the same way."

Claudia Muzio: "Every singer knows how important is the management of breath. I always hold up the chest, taking as deep breaths as I can conveniently. The power to hold the breath, and sing more and more tones with one breath, grows with careful, intelligent practice."

Frieda Hempel: "The very first thing for a singer to consider is breath control—always the breathing, the breathing. She thinks of it morning, noon and night. Even before rising in the morning she has it on her mind, and may do a few little stunts while still reclining. Then, before beginning vocal technic in the morning, she goes through a series of breathing exercises."

David Bispham: "Correct breath control must be carefully studied and is the result of understanding and experience. When the manner of taking breath, and the way to develop the diaphragm and abdominal muscles, is understood, that is only a beginning. Management of the breath is an art in itself. The singer must know what to do with the breath once he has taken it in, or he may let it out in quarts when he opens his mouth. He learns how much he needs for each phrase; he learns how to conserve the breath."

Oscar Saenger: "The management of the breath is a most important factor, as the life of the tone depends on a continuance of the breath. The student must cultivate the power of quickly inhaling a full breath, and exhaling it so gradually that she can sing a phrase lasting from ten to twenty seconds. This needs months of arduous practice. In all breathing, inhale through the nose."

Yeatman Griffith: "Breath control is indeed a vital need, but should not be made a bugbear to be greatly feared. Most students make breathing and breath control a difficult matter, when it should be a natural and easy act. They do not need the large amount of breath they imagine they do, for a much smaller quantity will suffice. When you open the lips after a full, natural breath, do not let the breath escape; the vocal chords will make the tone, if you understand how to make a perfect start."

Specific Exercises

Great singers are chary of giving out vocal exercises which they have discovered, evolved, or have used so constantly as to consider them a part of their own personal equipment, for reasons stated earlier in this chapter. However, a few artists have indicated certain forms which they use. Mme. d'Alvarez remarks, "When I begin to study in the morning, I give the voice what I call a massage. This consists of humming exercises, with closed lips. Humming is the sunshine of the voice. One exercise is a short figure of four consecutive notes of the diatonic scale, ascending and descending several times; on each repetition of the group of phrases, the new set begins on the next higher note of the scale. This exercise brings the tone fully forward."

Lehmann counsels the young voice to begin in the middle and work both ways. Begin single tones *piano,* make a long crescendo and return to *piano.* Another exercise employs two connecting half tones, using one or two vowels. During practice stand before a mirror.

Raisa assures us she works at technic every day: "Vocalises, scales, broken thirds, long, slow tones in *messa di voce*—that is, beginning softly, swelling to loud, then diminuendo to soft, are part of the daily regime." Farrar works on scales and single tones daily. Muzio says, "I sing all the scales, one octave each, once slow and once fast—all in one breath. Then I sing triplets on each tone, as many as I can in one breath. Another exercise is to take one tone softly, then go to the octave above; this tone is always sung softly, but there is a large crescendo between the two soft tones."

Kingston says, "As for technical material, I have never used a great quantity. I do scales and vocalises each day. I also make daily use of about a dozen exercises by Rubini. Beyond these I make technical exercises out of the pieces." Giuseppe de Luca sings scales in full power, then each tone alone, softly, then swelling to full strength and dying away. Bispham: "I give many vocalises and exercises, which I invent to fit the need of each student. They are not written down, simply remembered. I also make exercises out of familiar tunes or themes from opera. Thus, while the student is studying technic, he is acquiring much beautiful material."

Oscar Saenger: "We begin by uniting two tones smoothly and evenly, then three in the same way; afterwards four and five. Then the scale of one octave. Arpeggios are also most important. The trill is the most difficult of all vocal exercises. We begin with quarter notes, then eighths and sixteenths.

The trill is taken on each tone of the voice, in major seconds." Reinald Werrenrath: "I do a lot of gymnastics each day, to exercise the voice and limber up the anatomy. These act as a massage for the voice; they are in the nature of humming, mingled with grunts, calls, exclamations, shouts, and many kinds of sounds. They put the voice in condition, so there is no need for all these other exercises which most singers find so essential to their vocal well being."

J. H. Duval* asserts: "Long, sustained tones are too difficult for the young voice. One should sing medium fast scales at first."

LENGTH OF TIME FOR DAILY PRACTICE

It may be helpful to know about how much time the artists devote to daily study, especially to technical practice. It is understood all great singers work on vocalises and technical material daily.

Caruso is a constant worker: two or three hours in the forenoon, and several more later in the day, whenever possible. Farrar devotes between one and two hours daily to vocalises, scales and tone study; Lehmann counsels one hour daily on technic. Galli-Curci gives a half hour or so to vocalises and scales every morning. Martinelli practices exercises and vocalises one hour each morning, then another hour on repertoire: in the afternoon an hour more—three hours daily. Easton says, "It seems to me a young singer should not practice more than an hour a day, at most, beginning with two periods of fifteen or twenty minutes each." Anna Case says, "I never practice when I am tired, for then it does more harm than good. One must be in good condition to make good tones. I can study and not sing at all, for the work is all mental anyway." Muzio states she gives practically her whole day to study, dividing it into short periods, with rest between.

Frieda Hempel says, "I do about two hours or more, though not all of this for technic. I approve of a good deal of technical study, taken in small doses of ten to fifteen minutes at a time. Technic is a means to an end, more in the art of song than in almost any other form of art. Technic is the background of expressive singing."

Sophie Braslau is an incessant worker—"at least six hours a day. Of these I actually sing three hours. The first hour to memory work on repertoire. The second hour to vocalises. The rest of the time is given to repertoire and the things that belong to it." Barrientos states she gives about three-quarters of an hour to vocal technic—scales and exercises—each day. Duval advises the young student to practice two half hours daily, two hours after eating, and rest the voice one day each week, during which she studies

[*a young singing teacher in New York and Paris, briefly interviewed by Brower]

other subjects connected with her art. Oscar Saenger says, "One should practice in fifteen-minute periods, and rest at least ten minutes between. Sing only two hours a day, one in the morning and one in afternoon."

WHAT VOWELS TO USE

There seems a divergence of opinion as to what vowels are most beneficial in technical practice and study. Galli-Curci says, "In my own study I use them all, though some are more valuable than others. The "ah" is the most difficult of all. The "o" is good; "e" needs great care. I have found the best way is to used mixed vowels, one melting into the other. The tone can be started with each vowel in turn, then mingled with the rest of the vowels." Mme. d'Alvarez often starts the tone with "ah," which melts into "o" and later changes to "u," as the tone dies away. Bispham has the student use various vowel syllables, as: "lah," "mah," "may," and "mi." With Oscar Saenger the pupil in early stages at least, uses "ah" for vocalises. Duval requires students to use the vowel "ah" for exercises and scales, finding the others are not needed, especially excluding "e" and "u" as injurious. Griffith uses each vowel in turn, preceded by all the consonants of the alphabet, one after another.

HALF OR FULL VOICE?

Shall the young singer practice with half or full voice seems a matter depending on one's individual attainments. De Luca uses full power during practice, while Raisa sings softly, or with medium tone, during study hours, except occasionally when she wishes to try out certain effects. Martinelli states he always practices with full voice, as with half voice he would not derive the needed benefit. Mme. Easton admits she does not, as a rule, use full voice when at work; but, she adds, this admission might prove injurious to the young singer, for half voice might result in faulty tone production. Anna Case says that when she is at work on a song in her music room, she sings it with the same power as she would before an audience. She has not two ways of doing it, one for a small room and another for a large one. Mr. Duval advises the young pupil to sing tones as loudly and deeply as possible. Singing *pianissimo* is another fallacy for a young voice. This is one of the most difficult accomplishments, and should be reserved for a later period. Oscar Saenger: "The tone should be free, round and full, but not loud."

HEARING YOURSELF

"Does the singer really hear himself?" is a question which has been put to nearly every artist. Many answered in a comparative negative, though with qualifications.

Miss Farrar said, "No, I do not actually hear my voice, except in a general way, but we learn to know the sensations produced in throat, head, face, lips and other parts of the anatomy, which vibrate in a certain manner to correct tone production. We learn the *feeling* of the tone." "I can tell just how I am singing a tone or phrase," says De Luca, "by the feeling and sensation; for of course I cannot hear the full effect; no singer can really hear the effect of his work, except on the records."

"The singer must judge so much from sensation, for she cannot very well hear herself, that is, she cannot tell the full effect of what she is doing," says Anna Case. Mr. Witherspoon says, "The singer of course hears himself and with study learns to hear himself better. The singer should depend more on hearing the sound he makes than on feeling the sound. In other words, train the *ear,* the court of ultimate resort, and the only judge, and forget sensation as much as possible, for the latter leads to a million confusions."

VOCAL MASTERY, FROM THE ARTISTS' VIEWPOINT

Farrar: "A thing that is mastered must be really perfect. To master vocal art, the singer must have so developed his voice that it is under complete control; then he can do with it what he wishes. He must be able to produce all he desires of power, *pianissimo,* accent, shading, delicacy and variety of color."

Galli-Curci: "To sum up: the three requirements of vocal mastery are: management of the larynx; relaxation of the diaphragm; control of the breath. To these might be added a fourth: mixed vowels. But when these are mastered, what then? Ah, so much more it can never be put into words. It is self-expression through the medium of tone, for tone must always be a vital part of the singer's individuality, colored by feeling and emotion. To perfect one's own instrument must always be the singer's joy and satisfaction."

Raisa: "If I have developed perfect control throughout the two and a half octaves of my voice, can make each tone with pure quality and perfect evenness in the different degrees of loud and soft, and if I have perfect breath control as well, I then have an equipment that may serve all purposes of interpretation. For together with vocal mastery must go the art of interpretation, in which all the mastery of the vocal equipment may find expression. In order to interpret adequately one ought to possess a perfect instrument, perfectly trained. When this is the case one can forget mechanism, confident of the ability to express any desired emotion."

Homer: "The singer must master all difficulties of technic, of tone production in order to be able to express the thought of the composer and the meaning of the music."

Werrenrath: "I can answer the question in one word—Disregard. For if you have complete control of your anatomy and such command of your vocal resources that they will always do their work, that they can be depended on to act perfectly, then you can disregard mechanism and think only of the interpretation—only of your vocal message. Then you have conquered the material and have attained vocal mastery."

Kingston: "Vocal mastery includes so many things. First and foremost, vocal technic. One must have an excellent technic before one can hope to sing even moderately well. Technic furnishes the tool with which the singer creates his vocal art work. Then the singer must work on his moral nature so that he shall express the beautiful and pure in music. Until I have thus prepared myself, I am not doing my whole duty to myself, my art or to my neighbor."

Griffith: "Vocal mastery is acquired through correct understanding of what constitutes pure vowel sounds, and such control of the breath as will enable one to convert every atom of breath into singing tone. This establishes correct action of the vocal cords and puts the singer in possession of the various tints of the voice.

"When the vocal cords are allowed to produce pure vowels, correct action is the result, and with proper breath support, vocal mastery can be assured."

Duval: "What is vocal mastery? Every great artist has his own peculiar manner of accomplishing results—has his own vocal mastery. Patti had one kind, Maurel another, Lehmann still another. Caruso may also be said to have his own vocal mastery.

"In fine, as every great artist is different from his compeers, there can be no fixed and fast standard of vocal mastery, except the mastery of doing a great thing greatly and convincingly."

FRANCES ALDA *(1883–1952)*

MARGUERITE D'ALVAREZ *(1886?–1953)*

PASQUALE AMATO *(1878–1942)*

DAVID BISPHAM *(1857–1921)*

SOPHIE BRASLAU *(1892–1935)*   DAME CLARA BUTT *(1872–1936)*

ENRICO CARUSO *(1873–1921)*   JULIA CLAUSSEN *(1879–1941)*

FLORENCE EASTON *(1884–1955)*

GERALDINE FARRAR *(1882–1967)*

AMELITA GALLI-CURCI *(1882? 1889?–1963)*

MARY GARDEN *(1874–1967)*

ALMA GLUCK *(1884–1938)*

FRIEDA HEMPEL *(1885–1955)*

LOUISE HOMER *(1871–1947)*

LILLI LEHMANN *(1848–1929)*

DAME NELLIE MELBA *(1861–1931)*

CLAUDIA MUZIO *(1889–1936)*

ROSA RAISA *(1893–1963)*

ERNESTINE SCHUMANN-HEINK *(1861–1936)*

EMMA THURSBY *(1845–1931)*

REINALD WERRENRATH *(1883–1953)*

HARRY EVAN WILLIAMS *(1867–1918)*

HERBERT WITHERSPOON *(1873–1935)*